PRAISE FOR *STEADFAST PARENTING*

"*Steadfast Parenting* is easy to read, organized perfectly for parents of various aged children, and holds practical, immediately usable wisdom. *Steadfast Parenting* should become a daily companion for busy parents."—**Michael Gurian, *New York Times*–bestselling author of *The Wonder of Boys* and *The Minds of Girls***

"Patricia McGann's calm, knowledgeable, reassuring voice shines through this eminently practical guide to parenting an ever-growing child—from birth through the teenage years—in an ever-changing world. This will be the book that parents can turn to, again and again."—**Mary Quattlebaum, writing instructor/coach and author of *Jo MacDonald Saw a Pond* and *Adorable Animals***

"Patricia McGann's book is a treasure trove of outstanding advice, inspiring anecdotes, and personal testimonials. Her words ring true throughout. My own personal favorite aspect of the book, however, is her smart and sound advice about how to parent in a world of smart phones, social media, and modern-day materialism. You will look far and wide for wiser—or more helpful—words."—**Michael O'Hanlon, senior fellow and director of research, Foreign Policy Program, Brookings Institution**

"This book will provide insight and wisdom to everyone. McGann's writing style is honest, funny, and sometimes hard to hear. It is written with love, compassion, and understanding from a wonderful mom, wife, and educator."—**Susan M. Apgood, executive vice president, client relations, and founder of News Generation, Inc.**

"McGann is a once-in-a-generation leader. Her insight and perspective are well earned and invaluable."—**David Long, principal, Our Lady of Lourdes, Catholic School**

"Patricia McGann has captured what those who love children need to consider in order to truly care for them and help them blossom into their best selves. Her wisdom in these pages is invaluable."—**Doreen Engel, director of children and youth services, the Arc Montgomery County**

"McGann's poignantly written words provide the framework for cultivating individual works of art within the gallery of family and family values. McGann's wisdom from her years in education with her lessons learned from parenthood helps parents to 'be the parents that [our children] need us to be.'"—**Michelle C. Harmon, assistant principal, Montgomery County Public Schools, Maryland**

"Patricia McGann has combined her many years of education with an exhaustive list of real-life experience to craft a lighthearted, nonjudgmental, reassuring guide to parenting. Patricia's thoroughly entertaining, practical, and easy-to-read primer on parenting can bring out the best in any parent and child!"—**Joseph Dungan, trial court judge, prosecutor, trial attorney, father of four, grandfather of fourteen, and youth coach**

"As an educator with over thirty years of classroom teaching experience, I highly recommend *Steadfast Parenting*. It is a feel-good book that not only inspires parents but also gives them practical solutions for many of the common struggles parents experience. This simple, empowering book will help parents relax and enjoy the difficult yet rewarding journey of parenting!"—**Kathleen Dugan, teacher, Montgomery County Public Schools, Maryland**

Steadfast Parenting

How to Raise Children
of Character

Patricia McGann

ROWMAN & LITTLEFIELD
Lanham • Boulder • New York • London

Published by Rowman & Littlefield
An imprint of The Rowman & Littlefield Publishing Group, Inc.
4501 Forbes Boulevard, Suite 200, Lanham, Maryland 20706
www.rowman.com
86-90 Paul Street, London EC2A 4NE, United Kingdom

British Library Cataloguing in Publication Information Available

Library of Congress Cataloging-in-Publication Data Available

ISBN 978-1-4758-7323-8 (cloth : alk. paper) | ISBN 978-1-4758-7324-5

♾™ The paper used in this publication meets the minimum requirements of American National Standard for Information Sciences—Permanence of Paper for Printed Library Materials, ANSI/NISO Z39.48-1992.

Contents

Preface

You Got What You Needed: Can You See It?

Did you get a pianist when you were anticipating a star football player? Did you have your heart set on an academic superstar and find yourself with a child who couldn't care less about reading a good book? When you were expecting your first child, did you wish for a boy to throw catch with or a girl who would take ballet? Did you plan for a busy metropolitan life in a downtown condo and end up with a minivan and a house in the suburbs?

On those mornings when you are sitting in traffic for too long with one child who has to go to the bathroom, another who is worried about his perfect attendance record, and a baby who just wants to escape the car seat, do you wonder, "How did I end up here, when just yesterday all I had to worry about was what I would wear to work and how long the line would be at Starbucks?"

A few years ago, my dear friend was diagnosed with cancer. She had three young kids and was not at all ready to leave them. We realized that there would be no cure. In a quiet moment, she looked at me and said, "This was not the way I pictured this going." That made us both laugh and cry—the truth and the pain of it were almost too much. When I see her young adult children now, I know that they are just the kind of people she would have loved to be around. I wonder why God wouldn't let her be here to enjoy them, and then I remember: We don't get to decide.

There is a plan that will test our trust in ourselves and in our God, a plan that does not necessarily resemble our plan in the least. It may well be a plan that causes us sleepless nights, moments of excruciating pain, and overwhelming joy. While I wish someone could reassure me that things will work out, I have come to accept that sometimes I just have to hold on and ride it out.

Even today, when I look at our family picture, it takes me a minute to settle into the realization that, while it is not the picture I thought it would be, it is beautiful still. If we let them, those things that throw us for a loop are the same things that can bring us the most joy in our lives. So pull out a family picture and compare it with the one you thought you'd have. Then, be grateful that you got what you needed instead of what you asked for.

This book is my attempt to share the lessons I have learned—as one of thirteen children in a blended family, a wife of more than fifty years, a mother of four healthy children and one child whose body and brain were devastated when he was an infant, and the grandmother of fourteen. My career path looks more like a bowl of spaghetti—winding around and traveling off in many directions. I have been a psychiatric nurse; a gym, science, and reading teacher; a counselor; a high school administrator; a graduate school instructor; an elementary school principal; and an educational consultant. I hope you will accept these lessons learned and consider this book as a hand to hold while you travel the long, often delightful, and sometimes treacherous road that is parenting.

Just when we think we have things under control—just when we can see all our plans coming together—something wacky happens, and things start spinning off in every direction. That's when we are really tested. That's when we are forced to take a couple deep breaths and try to see the shine in the mess that is real life. And there is shine in it, and there is joy.

If you've ever done an art project with kids, you know that when all the paper and paint has been cleaned up, hands have been washed, and pictures taped to the fridge, evidence of your work remains—sometimes for months. It's the glitter, and it's everywhere—glitter on clothes, in the carpet, in your hair, and in the corners of the hardwood floor. Glitter shows up in the most surprising places. When you walk into a room or open a drawer, it shines in the corner of your eye—it sits on the periphery, asking us to pay attention.

Keep the glitter around as long as you can. It serves as a tiny, shiny reminder that asks us to look again, to take a second, to stop and pay attention because something important is happening, and we won't want to miss it. That's really the essence of this parenting job you've taken on—to be present for the small moments. If we can manage to avoid the avalanche of stuff that comes at us each day and keep our eyes on the incredible beings who have been gifted to us, we can be the parents that they need us to be.

This is tough work. You will make spectacular mistakes, and you will hit grand slams. Stay in the process, focus on your children, and leave the future to work itself out. Like you, I have been faced with challenges, some of which I have handled with grace, and some have knocked me right off my feet. I'm with you as you work your way through parenthood. Let's keep an eye out for one another along the way, and let's keep an eye out for the glitter.

Acknowledgments

Thank you, Mike O'Hanlon, for slogging through with me for all these months. Thank you, David Long, for sharing your remarkable insights. Thank you, Terry, Patrick, Kelly, Brendon, and Brighid, for teaching me what it means to be a good parent. Thank you, Mac. If you hadn't believed in me, I never would have done it.

Introduction

Have you felt like you are alone in your efforts to raise children with traditional values? If you are committed to raising young people of integrity and compassion, young people who demonstrate self-respect and respect for others as they contribute in a positive way to this world, you are not alone! This book was written just for you and for the many parents who refuse to let a materialistic, "me first" society steal the souls of their children. It is designed to meet you wherever you are in the process of parenting children, and it imparts lessons and advice for raising children of strong character in a world that sorely needs them.

Chapter 1 provides an overview of this most important, most incredible vocation you have chosen, this gift you have been given—the opportunity to raise a good person who will make the world a better place. Chapter 2 begins with the developmental tasks, the challenges, and the opportunities for character development that begin on the day baby comes home. Chapters 3 and 4 explore the family, social, and school life of children who are three to five years old. The family, social, and school life of children who are five to nine years old are presented in chapters 5, 6, and 7.

Chapters 8, 9, and 10 introduce us to the tumultuous and ever-changing terrain that is the world of tweens, ten to fourteen years old. Parents who want to emphasize respect and values as they discuss love, relationships, and sexual intimacy will find guidance and support here. The significant physical and social demands that exist for middle school boys and girls are discussed, and the subject of bullying is covered.

Chapters 11, 12, and 13 cover the teenage years and the challenges of maintaining a strong connection with your teen while encouraging his or her need for independence. These chapters discuss risk taking, reversing course, increasing responsibilities and privileges, what to do when things go wrong, and establishing house rules.

Chapter 14 is all about helping children to manage the stresses and grief that are part and parcel of family divorce. Chapter 15 covers executive functioning skills, which are necessary for academic success, and connects those skills with the stresses young people might face. A brief discussion of anxiety and depression, their signs and symptoms, and some ways to address them follows. You'll be reminded once again in chapter 16 to keep an eye out for the glitter as you engage in this incredibly important work that is raising children.

There are three lists at the end of the book that suggest things that your children should be able to do by the time they graduate from high school, the lessons you might want to impart to them along the way, and some good advice to give your children as you undertake this amazing job.

Chapter 1

Infancy to Young Adult in the Blink of an Eye

Every parent wants to do a good job raising his or her child. Much like other very difficult jobs, though, many people really struggle to get it right, and some quit trying to do it well because they didn't realize how hard it would be. It can be really tough to decide to put your own needs on the back burner and recognize that, as the adult, you have to reprioritize your life.

The truth is that when you're single and imagining "one day," or when you're newly married and planning for your future together, you likely have a movie-script vision of what it is like to create a family. Before you have your own children, you may feel free to make liberal use of the words *never* and *always* as you encounter and judge other families:

- "I will never let my kid act like that in public."
- "My child will always sleep in his own bed."
- "My child will always eat healthy meals."

Pre-parents read the books and feel quite confident about the task ahead, until those theoretical children are wailing at 4:00 a.m. or pooping all over the changing table. Pre-parent adults cannot imagine what it would be like to be that mom or dad waiting in line to pick up a prescription for a sick child while he screams unceasingly because he has an earache. They are also quite sure that a quick stop for fast food to keep a carful of children from melting down would never be an option they would choose.

It is frightening and demoralizing to find that you don't have the tools you need to raise your children the way you dreamed of raising them. It is tricky business trying to avoid the pitfalls that come with a firm vision of what you will do as a parent. You may be determined to grow a perfect child who gets good grades, acquiesces to every demand you make, scores at least one goal in every soccer game, and has tons of friends. In your mind, child-rearing is another project. You are very good at projects. You plan well; you implement very well; you collaborate, evaluate, revise; and you succeed. You know how you will organize and arrange things, maybe even work the system a bit to get the adult you want to have at the end of it all.

You may be determined to raise a young man who will play football, get a scholarship to Notre Dame, and then go on to law school. He'll want to join a lucrative private practice in the city so that he can buy a home for his family in the suburbs. After he is financially set, he can become a judge and serve out the last fifteen years of his career in beautifully furnished chambers, making well-reasoned decisions about other people's lives. You want him to be happily married, and to have a nice family. You want them to live near you and visit you at your Florida condo for a week every February. You're not planning for anything outrageous, but you know what you want for your son.

The trouble with this vision is that it can actually make you miss the joy and the heartache that will come from raising this unique child who's right in front of you. If you set unreasonable expectations and your son doesn't meet the milestones you have set, you will be disappointed in him. He will feel badly about that, and your disappointment will cause you to miss out on some very special moments in his life. You can plan and implement, collaborate and work the system to get your brilliant son to be that esteemed judge someday. But there is something else at work in your son's life. You might even find that out on that very first day, after a long hard labor, after all the dreaming and hoping for your son . . . your daughter will be born.

Once your child arrives and you have adjusted to the fact that she is a girl, you will raise her in the midst of a myriad of other demands. Financial, emotional, and relational issues arise. On an ordinary day, with the pings and rings of phones and work and family, it can be extraordinarily difficult to keep yourself present with your child when she needs you. You are up to your neck with responsibilities, so you make choices, and you prioritize. This may be the biggest choice of your life. You only have your children for a short time, and you want to make the most of that time—not so that you can grow a doctor or a lawyer but so that you can share the process of growing up with this incredible human you have been given.

You pause and enjoy the wonder he expresses at finding a beautiful leaf or a ladybug. You remember what it's like to get excited about something every single day. You spend twenty minutes walking one block, stopping to look at everything. You walk backward and sideways with your precious child. You skip and gallop, and you jump rope and play hopscotch. You have popsicles in the backyard, and your hands turn cherry red. You tell one another stories, and you read books over and over again until you both know them by heart.

Over time you realize that you aren't meant to gradually fade away from your child as he gets older. Instead, you are meant to adapt to his needs, staying constant in your love and your commitment to be there. You transition from your head-coaching position to the sidelines and eventually to the bleachers, but you remain tuned in, all in. He gradually takes over his own care; he makes his own choices; he creates his own vision of who he will be and how he will treat other people. Throughout the process, you remain.

As your child grows up, you show her what compassion, integrity, determination, faith, love, respect, and courage look like. You decide when to guide, when to give a little support, when to encourage, when to let her find her own way, and when you need to insist that she does things your way. It dawns on you that you have to live a life that will survive the scrutiny of some very astute observers—your own children. Sometimes you decide wrong, and you need to readjust, but you don't give up.

Gradually your role changes. Your almost-adult child sees you as a friend and teacher rather than as a boss. When things aren't going so well, your young adult may feel the need to turn his back on you, to separate from you. That's when your resolve will be tested, and your heart will break a little, but you stay with it—all in. You'll hold steady and be ready. You'll welcome him with open arms when he returns, but your relationship will once again be different. You might become a confidant and a trusted advisor, or for a while you may become a benevolent observer.

As you did when he was three and again at thirteen, you will adjust to your precious child, modifying your approach, as he needs different things from you. The one consistent in all of this will be your love for your child, and your commitment to be there when he needs you. No matter how old he gets, and no matter how competent she feels, they need to know that they can count on you.

This parenting business is not for the weak-kneed, but if you have faith, if you trust your instincts and keep an eye out for the shiny moments, you will do just fine.

IN THE MIDST OF IT ALL—UNTIL WE'RE NOT

There isn't a lot of time to consider the many choices that are required when you're a parent—to take a shower or a nap, to let an infant cry or pick him up, to use a time-out or a hug. While little babies are cute, they require constant attention at a time when parents are just getting used to the idea that they themselves are no longer their own first priority. Too little sleep and too many dirty diapers can push people right to the edge. Once children can get around on their own, the climbing, the running, the falling, and the bumps and bruises begin.

Language development is rapid-fire, and before you know it, you live with a person who says no to everything and has the ability to remember and repeat some of the most inappropriate comments you make. He only wants ice cream and grilled cheese, and she refuses to wear long pants in the middle of winter. You buy Disney Princess and Spider-Man underpants, and you wonder if your children will ever use the bathroom like normal human beings.

In the blink of an eye, though, they are donning Under Armour gym shorts, carrying lunch boxes, and refusing to kiss you goodbye in front of their friends. By the time they are in fifth grade, they are certain that they know way more than you do, and they love to challenge everything you say—usually in front of other adults. You worry about social media, cyberbullying, middle school sexuality, marijuana, alcohol, and fentanyl. It seems that there is always something new to worry about.

As they approach their teen years, you are painfully reminded of all the stupid and dangerous things you did when you were a teenager. The memories—some you didn't even know you had—can freeze you in your tracks. You decide before the first day of ninth grade that you will be tuned in, and you will not miss any of the clues that indicate trouble. You will make sure your teen knows she can talk to you about everything. You promise that you won't flinch, no matter the topic. You may even imagine yourself serving as a sounding board for some of your teenager's friends.

You've got this! That is, until your teenager answers you in one word, no matter the question, and refuses to ask you anything other than "What's for dinner?" or "Do you know where my phone is?" You're in control of the situation until you're not, until you discover that your child spends his evenings and often many hours in the middle of the night on Instagram or texting with friends.

This is not something you did. This is not something you will automatically know how to handle! How much is too much? Is this just a new version of talking to friends on the phone until all hours of the night? If you are paying attention, you will know if it is or not. You are torn between the desire to grab that phone and laptop and throw them right in the trash, and you fear that if you do, you might never see your kid again.

And then, once you've unpacked the car and arranged the belongings in the college dorm, it's time for you to walk away, wishing that you were secure in the knowledge that you have prepared your precious child for the future. You suddenly realize that what seemed like days that wouldn't end when he was two weeks old, two years old, then twelve, and then seventeen have gone by in a minute. You want to hold on, to hear one more endless story, wipe one more tear, tie one more shoelace.

On the ride home, you remember not the fights or the sleepless nights. You remember the homemade valentines, the spontaneous hugs, the projects you did together, the basketball games and the swim meets, the shopping trips, the Christmas mornings, the bedtime stories, and even those philosophical and political disagreements over dinner. You start to wonder,

- "Have we told her often enough that we love her?"
- "Does he know that we believe he is capable of amazing things?"
- "Will she find someone to eat dinner with?"
- "Will he remember to say his prayers?"

You wonder why you were always in such a hurry.

This is the time to trust that your best was good enough. When your child returns home at Thanksgiving, he will see you with new eyes—he will appreciate how much you love him and how much you did for him. And after a few days home, he will go back to school grateful that he will always have a safe place to return to—and just as grateful that you have given him the freedom to go.

There are lots of theories and philosophies about child-rearing available to parents. The science behind child development can provide valuable background information; the data collected by physicians, psychiatrists, and social scientists is interesting. The formulaic approaches to parenting promise to provide the simple answers to complicated parenting dilemmas. Parenting, though, is more art than science, and data and formulas don't necessarily translate into practice for parents who are in the midst of raising and teaching children. No theory, no program, no formula, no book can replace the instincts of a well-informed adult who loves his children, knows his own values and beliefs, and keeps his focus on what's happening right now.

One of the most essential tasks of this journey you are on is a review and articulation of your values and beliefs about the world in general and the importance of relationships. Think about how you see the world. While there is no doubt that the world does not currently provide a great environment for raising good citizens, do you still believe that people are essentially good?

Spend time considering whether the dreams and visions you have for your child are realistic or if maybe you should shelve them for a while. Maybe you should consider letting your child's life evolve as it will, with you guiding and supporting her as she develops her own interests and aspirations. When you focus on the process of parenting and growing, you aren't abandoning the dreams you have for your child (think, "My daughter will be a doctor"); you are just keeping those aspirations where they belong—on the horizon, which is a long way off. If you lose sight of the child in front of you because you are focused on the adult you want her to become, you confuse your child, and you guarantee that someone will be disappointed.

Children do not know and cannot imagine that there will be limits on what they can accomplish—and that's a good thing! Their hope for their own futures—tomorrow and in years to come—is brilliant, almost blinding. It is not your job to destroy or even shape that hope. It's not up to you to bring them down to reality or create a different dream for them. It's your job to teach your children how to live today so that they can create their own futures, futures founded on their own priorities and strong values.

> *When you improve a little each day, eventually big things occur . . . not tomorrow, not the next day, but eventually. Seek small improvements one day at a time. That's the way success happens—and when it happens, it lasts.*—John Wooden[1]

FOCUSING ON THE PROCESS

Parenting advice—books, columns, blogs, talk show experts—could we possibly hear any piece of advice about parenting that doesn't have an equally compelling opposite? Don't feed them that. Keep them away from this. Let them decide when and where they'll eat, what they'll play, how they will dress, or whether they want to obey. Get them involved in lots of activities. Let them roam the neighborhood alone. Don't let them out of your sight. Put them in your bed. Give them their own rooms. Sleep eight hours. Sleep when they feel like it. Go to school at age three. Delay kindergarten until they're six.

All of this advice is guaranteed to provide us with the end product that we should all be seeking—the perfectly behaved, brilliant, self-confident, well-adjusted, popular, very attractive young person who gets into the best high school in the area; is invited to take five AP courses freshman year; and goes on to a top-tier college, where he or she will be exceptionally well-prepared for law or medical school. Sadly, many parents today are focused on the product of their efforts. They can't help but feel inadequate or embarrassed if they don't grow children who meet the unreachable goals that the parenting gurus have set for them.

There was a time not so long ago when stay-at-home moms regularly got together with friends. They took their children for picnics in the park, field trips to the zoo, or just a day of play in the backyard. Because they were spending so much time together, they couldn't help but reveal their parenting flaws and faux pas to their friends. When mothers and fathers did or said something that was on the "don't do" list in Dr. Spock, they did or said it right in front of everyone!

Couples watched one another's kids during appointments or even for short trips. Teenaged babysitters were treasured, especially the ones whose parents didn't mind if they got home after 1:00 a.m. Being around other parents and their kids regularly provided everyone with a healthy perspective. There wasn't a perfect mother or father in the group. Everyone was doing their best, sometimes under pretty tough circumstances. Most of the time it was great fun, but even when it wasn't, parents had one another and a group of friends who got it.

As their children got older, mothers—some still in pj's and slippers—waved to each other in the carpool line in the mornings. They brought younger siblings to soccer practices and games and fed them McDonald's and pizza afterward. School communities became a source of support for families, and lifelong friendships developed—among children and among their parents.

Parents today have to work harder to enjoy the level of community that parents experienced twenty and thirty years ago. Today you can find yourself isolated and uncertain if you don't have opportunities to share the process with friends and family. You are rushing from work to school, to activities, to homework, baths, bed, and back again. It's not as much fun. It sometimes feels like people are judging (and sometimes they are), so nobody wants to share the stories of the messes and mistakes. It can be very lonely. With real effort you can create a small community of friends with whom you can share this adventure you're on, but it's worth the effort.

Look around when you're at the local park. Keep your eyes open as you attend events at school. You'll see that there are other moms and dads out there who don't always know what they're doing. There are other moms and dads who aren't reading their emails during the parent meeting. There are parents who look like they are enjoying their children. Make contact. Make the effort to build a small community around your children who will nurture them and support you.

Soon the parenting pundits will run out of things to say about the products parents are raising, and then moms and dads can get back to enjoying the experience—laughing and crying together, reminding one another that no one does this perfectly.

Chapter 2

Family and Social Life of Infants and Toddlers

When the nurses help you load that tiny infant into the brand-new car seat in your car, you can't help but wonder, "Are they crazy? Giving this baby to me? What do I do now?" Maybe during your pregnancy you read all the books and articles you could. You became an expert at being pregnant! Then, in the last month or two, you dove into the parenting handbooks. At the same time, other mothers and fathers might have felt compelled to give you their best advice:

- "Don't spoil him. Let him cry for ten minutes before you pick him up."
- "Start off right. Keep baby in your bed from the beginning."
- "Hire a nanny."
- "Find a day care center near your work."

At this moment you cannot remember anything you read or heard—not one single tip.

Early on, you can quickly lose track of hours and days. You're awake at 3:00 a.m. and dozing off at the kitchen table at 5:00 p.m. You feed the baby, change the baby, rock the baby, and do it all over again—over and over and over. You keep a detailed list of ounces in and poops out. You have no idea when you last showered.

You wonder when he's going to wake up and look at you. Three weeks later you wonder, "Why won't he sleep?" He doesn't sleep because the reality of his situation has sunk in. A doctor just yanked him out of his cozy cocoon, the only place he's ever known. He's trying to adjust to this drastic change. There is a lot to adjust to—the light, the intensity of sounds, the movement, the space. He needs time.

You rock him, you sing to him, you whisper to him, you wonder if any human ever smelled so good. You feel his breathing slow, and he snores just a tiny bit. You move incredibly slowly over to the cradle. Feeling an incredible strain in your lower back, you lift him into the cradle with excruciating care. You are engulfed by the overwhelming wave of love that comes over you. You are halfway down the hall to the shower when he begins to stir.

There is actually a good reason he stirs. You are not doing anything wrong. He is not doing anything wrong. There is nothing wrong. When you hold your baby and rock him and talk to him or sing to him, he settles in. His breathing matches yours. The warmth of his body on yours provides him with great comfort. The sound of your voice is familiar and soothing. He's been hearing it for nine months. When you move him away from you, he is startled. If you have help or if you can find help, then ask them to hold your baby while you shower. If you can't get another human, try using a sound machine that mimics the slow rhythm of a heartbeat, or record yourself singing quietly and play that while he sleeps. Use a piece of your clothing as a swaddle; the smell will be familiar.

Your baby sets the tone by needing the same things now that she will always need from you. She needs to feel that she belongs to you and with you—she needs to be attached to you. She needs to feel safe, which means she needs to know that you will come when she cries, that you will feed her and change her, and that you will keep her close to you.

Of course, your baby needs to feel loved. She needs your voice to be soft and your touch to be gentle. When you are exhausted and you've had enough, when you need a quiet lunch or a soothing shower, you need to let someone else hold your baby until you can regroup. If no one is available, then play some lullabies on your computer, settle baby in the crib, and give yourself a break.

It can help to remember that infants do not get spoiled by being held, nor will they be permanently scarred if they cry while you are in the shower. Babies are incapable of manipulating you or anyone else. They just need to be connected to you. Infants do not develop self-soothing behaviors by being left to "cry it out," but a fifteen- or twenty-minute break in a safe crib with soothing music or a sound machine will not cause your baby any harm.

The mundane exercises of diaper changing and feeding schedules can cause you to forget everything else—you might find yourself in the same sweatpants day after day after day. Sleep comes in sixty-minute blocks, and you are exhausted. Then, she smiles. She reaches her hands up to be held. You can prop her up in the high chair and give her a few Cheerios and a rubber spoon to chew on. You recognize that the world is a beautiful place again, and you feel your optimism returning!

Those first few months are a fog. Then the fog begins to lift. You take walks to the park, and she looks around. Then, graciously, she falls asleep on the way home so you can get that shower and maybe even make a phone call.

DAY CARE DECISIONS

Day care decisions can be difficult. There is nothing that works for all children and all families. If you plan to return to work after your maternity or paternity leave, you will want to have arrangements made far in advance so that you can spend your leave time with your new baby rather than on the phone, interviewing nannies, or trudging around to day care centers.

If you will be staying home with your baby, then you will want to know where the local parks are and whether there is a mothers' group in your neighborhood or development. You will still want to think about plans down the road. Some children are more than ready to expand their worlds by going to preschool when they are two or three. They enjoy the interaction with other children and learning new things in a more structured setting than you might have at home. Other children are perfectly content to stay home, take trips to the grocery store and walks to the park and the library, and go off to school when kindergarten calls.

If you will be working from home, then you will need to anticipate your baby's needs in advance. It is unrealistic to think that you will be able to take care of your child's needs and work full-time, unless you plan to spend a lot of evening and nighttime hours on your job. The stress created by trying to do both will likely make for a lot of frustration, exhaustion, and guilt.

Check out nearby elementary schools to see if they have day care centers. They are usually well staffed, well equipped, and not far from home. They are also more likely to allow you to sign up for a few days a week or half-days, if that works for your schedule. Maybe you can create an arrangement with another parent so that you can both work part-time and watch one another's children on off days.

There are pros and cons to consider in all childcare situations. If you decide to hire someone to care for your child at home, how will you ensure that time is scheduled every day for the activities that are important for his development? Choosing one person to spend all day with your precious child is a monumental task. Does the person share your philosophy of child-rearing? How will she handle it when your little one enters that obstinate stage, saying no to everything, stomping feet, and demanding?

As you consider this option, remember how easy it can be to get frustrated with an inconsolable baby or a two- or three-year-old, even when you love him more than life itself. Ask yourself if the person in front of you will handle your child with care and love even when he is not being all that lovable. If you hire a nanny, you must have absolute trust in her that she will love and care for your baby when no one is there to see what she does. On the positive side, your baby will be home, napping, eating, and playing in a familiar setting.

If your baby goes to a day care center, you will need to be prepared for snow day closings, sniffly noses, and the occasional bump or bruise. The upsides of the day care center are the extra attention and watchful eyes of a day care staff and the early socialization skills children develop in this setting. You'll need to know that the center doesn't have too many infants relative to staff and that infants are protected from curious toddlers. You will want to know if staff are willing to hold and rock a baby who needs comforting or if they believe that babies should cry themselves out.

In-home day care providers should meet certain licensing requirements, just as day care centers do. The difference is that they are not as visible to the public as centers might be. It is important to know who lives in and who visits the home where you leave your baby. Does the in-home day care provider have someone who substitutes for her or him periodically? Who is that person, and has he or she been screened and certified to provide care? Oftentimes, in-home day care is provided by a neighbor or someone parents have known for a long time. This can be reassuring and feel safe. There are, though, still lots of questions to be asked, no matter how awkward they might seem.

Some families have aunts and uncles or grandparents to provide care for their newest members. It is a true blessing for a child to have older relatives in their lives. It can be difficult for parents, though, if grandparents or other relatives begin to assume the parenting role for their children, even when they are home. In these situations, it is always a good idea to set the ground rules ahead of time and to be very clear about everyone's expectations. Will there be payment involved? What will happen if relatives want to take a trip or if they need an extra day off? Where will the care take place? Is care given in exchange for lodging? Will it be difficult, for example, for Grandmother to step back into her role of grandmother when the baby's parents are home? Or will she feel that, because she provides care all day, she should continue to have a say in how things are done when parents are home?

There are no hard and fast rules. With consistency and predictability as hallmarks, you can make the decisions that work best for your children and your family. Before the baby arrives, you can explore your options and talk to your pediatrician and people you trust. Then, you can make an informed decision. Always be prepared to be flexible, however. Sometimes, even when we do all the prep, things don't work out as we had hoped. That's why a strong plan B is always a good idea!

Preschool and day care meet the needs of working parents. Parents who work outside the home and the many who now work at home need their children to be cared for by nurturing adults during the day. Taking the time to carefully consider options is a very important step.

It might be very hard for you to leave your baby with others, and you can expect to worry about him at first. Your providers should be willing to answer your calls and emails and even send pictures during those early days, so that you can see that baby is fine. Your worry should lessen as you and your baby get into a good routine and as you receive daily updates about his day. If you are not comfortable with your day care provider, even if you're not sure why, trust your instincts and make a change.

PACING, PREDICTABILITY, AND FLEXIBILITY IN YOUR TODDLER'S DAY

Once she starts walking, the world expands—and she wants to see and touch it all. She opens cupboards and drawers. She is on the move. She grabs and chews on things that are just out of reach, or so you thought. Pots and pans, rubber spoons, plastic plates, and cups can all be very entertaining for your toddler. You can learn to step over and around her as she plays on the kitchen floor and you prepare a meal or do the dishes.

He goes up and down the stairs, teetering on the edge of the risers, scaring you to death. He can spend hours on the swing at the park. He has an incredible ability to notice the smallest things. He zooms in on the ordinary and finds the most extraordinary. If you stay with him, he can teach you to see things that you didn't even know you were missing—shiny things, tiny things, beautiful things. He runs at high speed from morning until night. Naptime is a treasure, but you have trouble deciding what to do with it. Should you make work calls, read the paper, take a nap, or make dinner?

She speaks baby talk and expects you to understand everything she says. The expression in her voice is incredible. She has private conversations with herself and her toys, and she asks questions. Your words and your responsiveness to her words provide the motivation for her to continue to express herself. When you use sophisticated vocabulary and abandon the need for baby talk, she will develop an expansive vocabulary of her own. As her language skills take off, you hear your words coming out of her mouth as she feeds her baby doll. You rediscover nursery rhymes and fairy tales that you loved as a child, and you share them with her.

Days for toddlers can and should be fairly predictable, regardless of their care situation. After a busy morning, they begin to wind down, and there is nothing better than story time to provide them with an opportunity to be still and regroup. Some children do well just spending time in their rooms or in a quiet corner with books and a few toys; others need a little more, and having stories read to them allows them to settle and fall asleep.

Whether it's every day or on your days off work, when your preschooler is at home, pacing is an important aspect of the day. If your life seems like a constant run—errands and jobs to get done, cooking and cleaning, and rushing to accomplish tasks—neither you nor your toddler will enjoy it much. You want to do what you can to make sure that she has enough time to play outside, some time with you (no matter what you're doing, she'll enjoy it), time alone to rest or look at books, and some time with others. This will help her learn to focus on one thing at a time.

While it all looks pretty simple to us, your preschool child is absorbing new knowledge all day long. Just as you learn best when you can stay with the task at hand, your young child will do the same. He will learn that every activity, every task, from getting up in the morning to going to the park, has a beginning, a middle, and an end. This is a great time to begin using the "First, then" phrase that you can use throughout your parenting life:

- "First we will put our shoes on, and then we will go to the park."
- "First we will brush our teeth, and then we will read a chapter in our book."

And in later years, it continues:

- "First I need you to help with the dishes, and then you can go out with your friends."

"First, then" reminds parent and child that responsibilities and privileges are always connected.

Preschoolers are constantly learning. They are consumed by curiosity, and within the context of a normal day, they can have lots of opportunities to expand what they know even as you accomplish the things you need to do. Trips to the grocery store or a walk to the post office or local coffee shop can be wonderful adventures—as long as you're willing and able to take your time. An hour at the local library for toddler reading time allows your little one to enjoy the company of other children and explore the world of books. Let your toddler pick one or two books from the children's shelves, take them home, look at the pictures, and read them. Even when you are positive those books are not books he will enjoy, go ahead and take them home anyway. You can check out some books you're sure he will love, and once you get home and start reading, it won't matter who picked out what.

Discovering an earthworm or examining a shiny pebble, watching the trucks at a construction site, sitting on a bench and watching people rush back and forth—all these simple experiences provide a great opportunity for your child to learn about the world around her. If you talk about what you see and hear as you watch the world, you will join her in noticing all kinds of cool stuff. Noticing is a huge part of learning, and it strengthens and sustains her natural curiosity.

When children know what's coming, they can participate in daily activities far better. Everyone has heard the overtired child wailing in the shopping mall as his mom just tries to make one more stop. You will need to learn about his tolerance level, and you will need to learn to respect nap times. Your schedule is no longer yours alone. At the same time, if you are flexible, you can teach your child to be flexible. When the schedule changes, you might say, "Even though we usually go to the library on Saturday mornings, this week we are doing something different. Because your cousins are in town, we're going to go to the zoo with them instead."

TERRIFIC TWOS AND THREES, FANTASTIC FOURS

There are certain times when a two-year-old just doesn't want to cooperate. As she gains language skills, one of her first words is usually *no*. She will use it a lot. When you try to interrupt her play to change her diaper, she will not cooperate. Trying to talk her into cooperating is not always the best option. The time and energy you spend explaining that a wet diaper is not good for her skin and that it smells bad could be used more productively. Too much talk when your toddler is wailing can actually escalate her hysteria.

Try doing something silly, like putting the clean diaper on your head while you get her pants off. Sing a very quiet song when she screams. She will quiet down to hear. Move quickly and calmly. The diaper will get changed, the baby will smile again, and she will move on. These jumps from joy to misery and back again can take place hourly in the life of the toddler.

When he's having a great time in the bathtub but it's time to get out, you can anticipate a struggle. You can just charge in and remove him, and sometimes that's the only option because you're in a hurry and you're tired. He will likely get angry and upset. Unfortunately, the tears and the struggle pretty much erase all the fun he just had, and that can make it harder to get ready for a peaceful bedtime.

If you can give yourself a minute and pull out the stopper while he is still in the tub, you might find that things move more quickly later on. He might not be crazy about that idea, but he can at least watch the water go down, line his toys up on the side of the tub, and discover on his own that bath time is over. He can "decide" that he might as well get out of the tub because it's cold and no more fun.

Giving toddlers choices can eliminate lots of struggles, as long as you give smart choices. Limit the options to two or three, and he will feel like he has some control. Both of you will avoid tears most of the time, although it's important to remember that tears are an important part of a toddler's life. They are his way of communicating his needs, his disappointments, his fears, and his confusion. Your mission should not be to eliminate all tears and frustrations from your toddler's life. That's destined to fail, and it's not particularly good for him to learn that you will make everything right for him no matter what.

When you give your toddler choices, ask her to tell you why she chooses one thing or another. This gives her a chance to consider her choices and begin to understand that there is a process to choosing what we want to do. This can also limit the number of times your child decides she doesn't really want macaroni and cheese after you've prepared it or strawberry yogurt after you've purchased it.

"Why did you pick these shoes today? Do you want to wear your boots today? I heard it might rain." If she chooses to wear the purple socks with the red pants, then compliment her choice and ask her how she decided on such a nice color combination. She might just answer, "I like purple," but that's perfectly fine. She's thinking.

Letting a four-year-old know ahead of time that he will be able to choose one thing from the cookie aisle or the bakery counter at the grocery store will help to avoid the otherwise frustrating battle centered around a child wanting every bag of Doritos or every candy bar he passes. Sticking to the "one choice" routine every single time you go to the store is important. Consistency is key!

FOOD FIGHTS

Mealtime with preschool children is always an adventure. You've received all the warnings about feeding your children only organic foods, avoiding or introducing peanut products, avoiding or pushing dairy, and avoiding all sugar and processed foods. You've heard it all, and there are enough opinions about what to feed kids out there to freeze you in your tracks.

Your pediatrician can provide you with guidelines, and you can adjust those guidelines to meet the needs and habits of your family. Once you've decided what to feed him, you have to figure out how to get him to eat. Whenever you can sit with your children at mealtime, you should. This is an opportunity to nourish the body and soul, to strengthen family ties, and to teach manners. Just don't try to do all of that in one or two sittings a week.

Establishing routines around the meals that your child eats at home can help the whole family enjoy being together and sharing a meal. Everybody needs their own seat, including your youngest member, be it a high chair pulled up to the table or a booster seat. Everyone needs a plate and utensils and a napkin, even if someone doesn't always use hers. Your toddler will probably fight you like crazy if you try to wipe her face every few minutes during a meal, but often she will gladly take a swipe at her face with her own napkin if you suggest it.

If you prepare a balanced meal for the family, your toddler can eat what you eat with few exceptions. He won't necessarily want to eat what you eat, but if that's what you prepare, you should give it to him. Children are not miniature adults, and so reasoning with him to try something is fruitless. If you encourage him to try the food and he won't, leave it be. Eventually, after seeing it on his plate ten or twenty times, he might give it a taste, or he might never eat it, no matter how many times he sees it there. It is a mistake to replace broccoli with yogurt if broccoli is on the menu and yogurt is not.

You will worry that she isn't getting enough to eat if she refuses half of what's on her plate. Give her time. She won't starve, and her refusal is more about establishing her independence than it is about eating. If she only eats the chicken tonight, tomorrow night you can offer fish, yogurt, broccoli, and carrots. That way you know she's getting enough, and she still gets something she likes and maybe something that she hasn't tried before. Ketchup and anything else that can be used as a dip will help. Dipping is fun.

As your toddler gets older, she will model her eating habits after yours if there is not a lot of drama around what she eats and doesn't eat. Try to keep it light, and dinner will be pleasant for everyone. When she throws the broccoli on the floor, don't give it back. Just pick it up, throw it away, and get on with your dinner. No response will eventually result in no repeat of the behavior.

It might seem like a good idea to promise ice cream or a cookie if your four-year-old will eat his green beans, but all that does is reinforce the idea that green beans are yucky and sweets are great. Instead, try your "first, then" method: "First we will all eat our dinners, and then we will decide what to have for dessert. What do you think Dad will pick, a cookie or ice cream?"

If your dinner conversation with older children or other adults goes long, it is best to release your toddler to play after about fifteen to twenty minutes so that his meal ends peacefully and yours can continue without upset. Asking your preschooler and older children to help you prepare some part of the meal will give him a stake in the meal and may encourage him to eat what is prepared.

Toddlers and elementary school children need to be offered three meals and at least two snacks a day. A healthy snack, like carrots and hummus or apples and peanut butter, in the late afternoon will help to change the tenor of that

difficult hour before dinnertime when she is tired and hungry and can't find
anything to do but whine.

DIVERSION AND DIRECTION

When you tell a toddler, "Don't jump on the couch!" she will hear, "Jump
on the couch." Instead, try rewording your instruction: "Please jump on the
trampoline or on the floor."

When your preschooler is insistent about pulling everything out of the
toybox and playing with nothing, you have some choices to make. If it's the
twentieth time he's done that today, you might have come to the end of your
rope; you might hear yourself saying, "If you don't stop that, I'm going to
take all the toys and put them away until you know how to play with them
properly!"

Instead of the empty threat, you could use this as an exercise in organizing. Once the toys are all over the floor, take a few minutes, sit down, and
start categorizing them. Put the trucks in one pile, the blocks in another pile,
the instruments in another pile, and the dolls in another pile. Talk about what
you're doing, quietly and slowly. Once you have his attention, put something
in the wrong pile. See if he notices. You could also sort them by color or size.
It's not the end of the world if they remain on the floor for a while, especially
if the two of you have had some positive moments sorting them.

You could also choose to make your life easier by waiting until he's in
bed and then removing all of the toys from the toybox. Replace only four or
five toys. Put the rest away for a couple of weeks, and then switch them out.
Two weeks later, you will have another small group of toys, and then you can
begin the rotation all over again. This way, his toys seem almost new after he
hasn't played with them for a while. It also makes the cleanup easier if you
don't have to put fifty toys back every time he feels like pulling them out.

While this may seem like a major inconvenience, it's important to remember that teaching and guiding your child is your most important job now. Give
it the attention it deserves. The laundry and dishes will wait.

Shannon

Shannon, a precocious two-year-old, loved pulling all the Pampers out of
the huge bag her mom bought at Costco. She somehow always managed to
get the bag open while her mother was carrying in all her other purchases.
By the time Mom finished carrying things in, Shannon had scattered the
one-hundred-pack of pull-ups all over the family room floor, and Mom was
in danger of falling over them.

Shannon's mom, being the clever mom she was, devised a great game. They would count out groups of ten because that was how high Shannon could reliably count. After they counted to ten, Shannon would carry those ten to a designated spot. Ten to the downstairs changing table, then ten to the diaper bag, ten to the changing table in the baby's room, and on and on until all the Pampers were put away. Shannon got some great counting practice. The Pampers got put away. Nobody fell over them, and most important, Shannon and her mom spent a very precious half-hour together.

Henry

Henry was a good boy. Periodically, he had trouble following instructions from his mother. At his fourth birthday party, Henry decided it might be fun to taste the bubbles. As he put the little blue bottle of bubbles to his lips, his mom hollered from across the yard, "Henry, don't drink the bubbles!" Henry drank the bubbles, and Henry threw up. The party wasn't much fun for Henry after that.

A few months later, Henry was playing in the basement. Somehow he got the lid off of a can of paint. His mom came down to find him with a big smile on his face, holding the can in his chubby little hands. Because she had not yet learned her lesson, Henry's mom called out, "Henry, be careful not to spill that paint!" as she walked toward him. Henry poured the paint out on his clothing and the basement floor. Even Henry was pretty shocked at the result. He dropped the can and tried to extricate himself from the pool of paint, but he kept slipping and falling, right into the paint.

When his mom finally managed to get Henry out of the paint, they were both covered. She placed Henry right into the laundry tub, where the washer hose drained on him just at that moment. Henry was not a happy guy. Henry's mom wasn't too happy either, although she might have smiled when the water splashed all over Henry. Hours later, after shampoos and baths, they sat down to talk about what had happened.

Turns out Henry heard, "Spill that paint." Henry's mom learned that she needed to readjust her instructions to Henry, especially when she felt frantic about what he might do and when she raised her voice. After that, when she needed to keep Henry from disaster, his mom approached him calmly and slowly, despite her desire to rush to the scene. She made eye contact with him and offered him an alternative. "Henry, let's put the can down and find a paint brush so we can paint some boards with it" would have worked wonders.

Being at home with your preschoolers allows you to watch *Sesame Street* together and clean the house at the same time. It takes longer with their help, but what's the rush? Running errands on your days off from work with a little companion who is pretty much interested in everything you want to do can be fun. It can take a while for you to get comfortable with slowing yourself down and limiting errands and chores, but really, who cares if you get all your tasks done on Saturday? Even if you work during the week, make sure that you take your toddler with you when you head to the store or out for errands on the weekends. Those are precious hours that you will be glad you spent with him.

POTTY TRAINING

No one knows the best way to potty train your toddler, no matter how many books have been written about it. Do you let the child decide when and where? Do you set a timer for every thirty minutes and then rush him into the toilet? Maybe you sit her on a little plastic potty and let her watch cartoons until she goes. Then you go wild with celebration and hand out the M&Ms.

Is the ideal age for potty training twelve months, eighteen months, or three years? Do you just have to make sure she's potty trained before she starts kindergarten? Some people think you should sit the toddler on the toilet with music or an iPad. Others sing "poop" songs and watch videos. Some children who are potty trained during the day continue to wear pull-ups at night until they are six or seven, just in case. Loading kids up with water might make it easier to get them to go. Running water in the sink while they sit there might help. Who knows?

What works like a charm with child number 1 will be an epic fail with child number 2. Some kids want to be potty trained, some kids think they want to be potty trained until they don't, and some kids simply don't. Only a parent who pays attention will know when to try—the first time, the second time, or the twentieth time. The last thing you want to do is begin a cold war with your toddler over potty training (or eating).

The timing of potty training will depend as much on your schedule as it does on your child's readiness. You might start potty training your child so that she is trained before she begins preschool, or you might decide to accomplish the task during the summer, a long weekend, or your vacation time. You might decide to put your little one on the potty every thirty minutes every day for five days. When she goes you can celebrate, and when she doesn't you can just move on. Even after an intensive introduction to potty training, there will be accidents.

If there are frequent accidents or if there are tears whenever you mention using the potty, it's time to take a break. If your child refuses to poop on the potty and becomes constipated, the tears and anxiety level will increase. Time to take a break and give everyone a chance to reconsider. Two- to three-year-olds who are in day care settings will very likely be taken to the potty regularly and usually all together. This will normalize the process for children and make it easier for your child to get a routine down—at least at day care. Again, this may not transfer to the home setting because oftentimes potty training for a two-year-old becomes about the ability to say no and the need for some autonomy.

Quietly mentioning that you are going to the bathroom when you go and calmly asking if he would like to go at the same time might eventually encourage your little guy to try again. Having a very visible bowl of M&Ms near the potty might work, as well. At the beginning, a reward for sitting for fifteen minutes regardless of results might encourage regular visits. At some point you will be lucky enough to get results, and that's when the cheering kicks in.

Telling your child that you want no more accidents is like telling someone not to trip and fall. Accidents are just that—accidental. Patience, new underpants, verbal reassurance that this will work just fine eventually, and a calm and accepting demeanor will allow both you and your child to get to the endpoint you seek without being traumatized.

BECOMING A BIG BROTHER OR SISTER

A toddler who will soon be an older sibling may need to get established in a preschool or day care program, be comfortable, and look forward to going every day. That way he will not be reluctant to depart the home when his sibling is curled up on your lap. While he may not be crazy about the idea that you and baby are home without him, by then he will love playing with his friends and having adventures with his teachers.

Preparing number 1 will be important, too. Letting him know what will happen will ease some of the natural anxiety that might arise when suddenly you are not at home. You might say, "When the baby is ready to come, we will call Nana, and she will come and stay with you. Mom will go to the same hospital where I went when you were born, and I will come home a couple days later with your new sister. You won't have to miss school because Nana will take you while we are gone, and when we return, we will soon be back in our routines. You will go in the morning and come home in the afternoon. When you get home, you will have a snack, and then you will have time to play before dinner and your bath. Mom will read you your stories before bed, and we will tuck you in, just like always."

While this might seem like a lot, it is simply a recap of all the routines he's used to. This information should be shared regularly before baby comes. It will reassure number 1 that his life will not be turned upside down because of the new arrival. You know, of course, that it will certainly be different, but the transition can be gradual and thus easier for him to accept. By the time the baby is fully awake, and more demanding of attention, her older brother will be able to hold her (with supervision) and talk to her. The bonding will begin, and it will be harder for him to wish her gone.

When you introduce a new sibling to toddlers and preschoolers, you may feel sorry for your number 1 baby, and you may feel guilty. Don't let your guilt push you to overindulge your toddler, responding to every tantrum with rewards and affection. Keep up your routines and encourage him to keep eating and using the potty. If he has accidents, don't panic. Just say, "Uh-oh, let's get changed."

Try giving her some jobs. This will allow her to maintain connection to you as she adjusts to the fact that she is now sharing her parents with a stranger. Having her pick out clothing for the baby or sending her for a clean blanket for the baby gives her something positive to do. Ask her if she thinks the baby is hungry or wet when the baby cries.

Make every effort to keep her routines in place when her new sibling arrives. This will be reassuring. If she goes to day care or preschool, make sure she continues to go. Remind her that you will see her when she gets home and that you two will have your usual walk to the park when she arrives. Try your best to spend at least thirty minutes of alone time with your toddler each day.

There is no doubt that your toddler will be a little sad when he recognizes that this small visitor will not be leaving any time soon. He will miss his status as the star of the show, and it will take some time for him to adjust to the new situation. Even at this early point in his life you can help him to see things with an optimistic lens. To do that, you can create situations where he can experience success and feel good about what he has done.

Help him to clean up his toys, and cheer like a crazy person when the job is done. Teach him to put his own coat or socks on, and tell Grandma all about it, so he can celebrate the accomplishment. Be an optimist yourself. Talk about all the wonderful things he and his new sister will do when they get older.

GUILT

Guilt can be a destructive force in the life of a family. It serves no purpose for parents to mire themselves in guilt because they've made a mistake or because their children seem to need far more than they can give. Your children will not be shortchanged if they don't have the newest toys or don't get to go to Disney World. They will be shortchanged if you spend your time beating yourself up because you don't give them what they think or you think they need. They need one thing more than anything else, and that one thing can erase all the missteps and make up for all the things they cannot have, for whatever reason: They need you, simple as that. They need to know you love them unconditionally and that you will guide them and love them all the way through.

Anticipate good things every day, and do that out loud. Even when you are tired and wondering what you've gotten yourself into, you can fake it if you have to and muster up some optimism for your precious child.

Bennie

Bennie was the fourth of four boys. Bennie had a raspy voice and a stout little body. He often played with Fisher-Price characters that he called his "guys." Bennie's imagination was strong. The conversations his "guys" had were amazing, and his mom loved to listen in from the other room. When he was four, Bennie began to talk about his "long-time-ago friend." The friend did not have another name, but Bennie knew a lot about him.

If someone was talking about skiing at the dinner table, Bennie would pipe up with, "My 'long-time-ago friend' liked to ski." His friend knew lots of things and did lots of things. Bennie would point to Greenland on the globe to show his family where his long-time-ago friend lived. He showed them Greenland every time, although he did not know the name Greenland. By the time Bennie was six, he didn't talk about his friend anymore, but his mom smiled when occasionally she heard Bennie talking to his friend as she listened from the other room.

Because no one ever challenged Bennie on the existence of his long-time-ago friend, because his parents and siblings enjoyed hearing the stories Bennie told about his friend and got a kick out of the fact that Bennie wasn't shy about sharing his stories with them, Bennie was able to enjoy the company of his imaginary friend without feeling like it was silly or wrong to have an imaginary friend. With three older brothers, it would seem that Bennie didn't need anyone else to talk to, but clearly, he found pleasure in having a friend who listened to everything he said. Eventually, he outgrew the need for his long-time-ago friend, and he was able to say goodbye to him on his own time.

From the very beginning, if children experience unconditional love, tender care and guidance, and a shared, unbridled enjoyment of every day, they will begin the process of becoming confident, contributing members of your family and their school communities. The key is to treat time with your little one(s), no matter how much you have, with the reverence and respect that it deserves. This is early in the process, but you are setting the foundation for everything that follows. What you do in those first five years matters. Your children need to know that you want to be with them and that you will be with them no matter what. Listen to their stories, ask questions, tell them stories about themselves and the day they were born. Sing to them, rock them, and kiss and hug them.

Chapter 3

Family and Social Life for Three- to Five-Year-Olds

No matter what your family looks like, it is within your family that your three- to five-year-old child discovers thousands of things about the world and many things about herself and the people around her. She begins to understand the concept of family; again, no matter what her own family looks like, to her it's the norm. Children begin to understand that, while they are loved immensely, they are not the center of the universe. They are members of a family group that supports itself and its members.

GROWING INTO FAMILY

At home your three- to five-year-old can begin to take on some responsibilities for his own care, and he can contribute by participating in household chores. This is the time when a five-year-old learns what it means to "clean your room" or "clean up your toys," if (and that's a big if!) you take the time to do these tasks with him.

Oftentimes parents find themselves telling their children, "Clean up your toys," several times and getting a totally blank look in response, and then they end up picking them up themselves. The only thing kids learn from this experience is that you'll do it for them. If you take a few minutes to join them in the process—showing them how to put the cars in one bin and the blocks in another and praising every effort—toddlers will pitch in. So instead of cursing at 9:00 p.m. when you're tired, you step on another block, and you have to get down on your hands and knees to throw everything into the toy box, make a resolution to do things differently. Try taking twenty minutes the next evening to work with your child to put things away. It is worth it in the long run.

When his room needs straightening, try this. "First, let's put your coat in the closet. Then, let's decide which clothes are dirty. Should we sniff them or study them for spots? Now, let's put the dirty clothes in the hamper and the clean ones in the dresser." Asking, "Where would you like to put your dolls?" allows your child to have some control over the process, and if you can hold your tongue when your son wants twelve superheroes in the bed with him, he will eventually learn on his own that he's more comfortable with only one or two.

After working together on the clean-room project for a few months, you can gradually withdraw your support, maybe getting things started and staying nearby in case he forgets or gets distracted. This time taken early on is well worth it because when you tell your eight-year-old to clean his room, he knows exactly what the process entails and what a clean room looks like.

MELTDOWNS

Your child will likely experience some incredible meltdowns. When she is tired, when she is confused about what you want from her, when she is clear about what she wants but can't get it, she will often melt down. Sobbing, screaming, stomping feet, and even swinging fists will let you know that your little one is terribly unhappy. Losing your temper when she refuses to put on her pajamas or comes out of her room five times after you've tucked her in tells your child a couple of things. First, she learns that she can regain control of the situation just by sending you over the edge. Second, she learns that, when things go wrong, it might be useful to start screaming and yelling.

If these meltdowns occur in public, it can be embarrassing, and you can find yourself unsure about what to do. What if, despite all your good preparation, a meltdown takes place in the checkout line at the grocery store? Do you ignore it and hurriedly get the groceries paid for and get out of the store? Do you leave everything on the belt and run for the door? Do you give her whatever it is she wants because you cannot bear the stares and the comments of the strangers around you? Or do you quietly speak to your screaming child, telling her that the screaming is upsetting the people around her, and that she already knows she cannot have whatever it is she wants?

It depends on your level of patience and your ability to withstand the public reaction to your child's histrionics. Ideally, you get your groceries paid for, and you and your little angel get to the car as quickly as possible. Once you have wrestled her into her car seat and you've loaded up your groceries, you take a deep breath, and you drive. Maybe you turn on some gentle music. You don't talk unless it's absolutely necessary. Let her work through it. Let her fall asleep if she can. If she does, maybe drive around for a while.

AFTER-INCIDENT REVIEW

Children in this age group have short memories when it comes to their own behavior. At the same time, they do not often forget what you tell them. It will be helpful for you to figure out what went wrong—if anything. Was your daughter simply overtired? If so, you will plan the timing for the next trip to the grocery store better. Did she not understand that she could only choose one thing? Did she think that she could change her mind on the *one thing* at the last minute? Could you have let her do that? She normally enjoys going with you, so don't abandon the idea of taking her; just plan better.

Once you have reviewed the situation in your own mind, it is a good idea to ask her a few questions about what she thought or understood but only after she has moved on from the upset. A few casual questions might help, but don't replay the horror. Rather, ask her what she thinks happened, and give her some options: "Do you think you were just too tired for grocery shopping yesterday, or did you not understand the 'buy one thing' rule? What were you trying to tell me when you were so upset?" Once you have what she offers and you have reviewed what you might do to make the next shopping trip more pleasant, leave it.

TIME-OUT

Time-out is a tricky proposition. If you use time-out to cool down—either for you or your child or both of you—it can be a perfect move. It is important to make sure your children know that's why you're calling time-out. Using a sports analogy might help: Coaches call time-out when the game is getting exciting and the players need to calm down and make some plans for next steps.

If time-outs are used as a punishment, they remove your children from the one person they really need when their feelings are threatening to overwhelm them. Far better to say, "I think we both need a break to calm ourselves down and think about what is happening," rather than an angry, "Go to your room!"

A quiet calm tone can help you both back off and regroup. Let your child know that you understand he is upset because he can't have what he wants; at the same time, it may help to let him know that it's your job to take good care of him and teach him how to act. Any prolonged conversation about whatever caused your little one to lose control is a waste of time and energy.

In the simplest terms, when your children are young, they need to learn how to act, and you are responsible for teaching them how to act. Children are not born knowing the rules, and they will pick up some rules of living by watching how the adults in their lives treat one another and how they treat friends and strangers. You will need to make the effort and take the time to teach children directly and with clarity how to act. This is not a one-time lesson. This is every day, all the time. It's who you are and how you interact. Defiant behavior is natural in preschoolers, and it may seem unimportant, but if you don't deal with it in some way, it will continue long past the age when it is expected.

You don't want to be the master of excuses for your child, explaining away every misbehavior, but you also understand that they are not born knowing the rules and that they have to figure out how those rules apply in new situations all the time. By balancing the need to correct poor behavior and recognizing that children will make mistakes, you can usually come up with an appropriate response when your children err.

CONSISTENCY

Forgive them quickly when they embarrass you with a meltdown, and acknowledge that everyone has bad moments, hours, days. Do not withhold your love and affection as a punishment for bad behavior. Love your little one when he's acting like he's possessed as much as you love him when he snuggles in for a story and gives you a kiss on the cheek.

GETTING ALONG WITH OTHERS

If your son doesn't play well with other children because he wants to control every aspect of the game and wants to use a toy or a piece of equipment as soon as he sees another child has it, he can quickly become isolated from other children. They will either be afraid of him, physically defend themselves, or smart enough to play where he cannot get to whatever it is that they have. His behavior is the result of an inability to adjust cognitively to the increasing demands that come with being around other children. You will need to be specific and concrete as you teach him to play and interact in an acceptable way.

You may want your little one to have friends, but he may not be ready to cooperate and collaborate yet. He may still be at the stage where he needs to learn to parallel play; he can be in the same space as other children and even play with some of the same toys, but he doesn't yet know how to exchange toys or work together with his peers on a task.

Forget about telling him to "think about how that makes Susie feel" when he grabs a toy from her. Empathy is not even on your son's radar. He does not have the cognitive capacity to understand how Susie feels. He might mimic your language and say, "Sad," but he doesn't really get it. Instead, focus on the rule that we can't grab from one another. Focus on the art of taking turns and diversionary tactics. Angrily taking the toy away will confuse your child, and he will cry because you've just done to him what he did to Susie. A brief explanation of the rule that "we don't grab from someone else" and the offer of a similar toy to both children, giving Susie first pick, will usually allow them both to move on.

A child who gets upset when asked to share toys or to wait for a turn needs some practice. You can practice taking turns and sharing with your child at home. Play some simple board games, and don't always let her win. Build with blocks and offer to trade one of your blocks that she might need with one of hers. Color some pictures, using one box of markers. You will both need that one red marker eventually. Work it out with her so that she can see the benefits of sharing.

Punishing your little one for being selfish or stubborn will not affect a positive change in her behavior. Modeling good behavior and positive interactions will teach her that there is a right way to get along with others.

If, though, you allow your four-year-old to take things from other children and do not teach her how to wait in line or take turns, she will certainly struggle when she enters elementary school. Teachers and other children will not always allow her to have her way. They will expect her to cooperate and collaborate. They will ask her to take turns and stand in line and wait.

This is the time to prepare your child, understanding that these skills are not developed overnight and that they do not come naturally to three-year-olds who are exclusively focused on their own needs and desires. Sometimes this will require a simple and straightforward *no*, and sometimes it will require that you remove him from a situation where he might hurt another child.

You will then have to bear up under the fury and the tears that will often accompany you taking control in these difficult situations. If you remain calm, speak in a very quiet and measured tone of voice, and express an understanding of your child's frustration, things will run their course. Long discussions and explanations will not help the situation. Be patient and present, and you can wrap the whole mess up with a hug and a couple of books before bed. While it might be tempting to rehash the situation after he has calmed down, resist the temptation. It will serve no purpose. With children this age, once it's over, it's over.

EXPERIENCING THE LARGER WORLD WITH YOU

There is nothing inherently wrong with making your life more convenient. The use of meal plans, Amazon Prime, phones that allow email access, Peapod, dog walkers, personal trainers, house cleaners, and decorators all provide you with more time to do the important things in life, right? Not always.

The preoccupation with the easier and more convenient steals the shiny stuff from your family life. You and your child miss those moments and hours that are spent together working on something—making dinner, washing the dog, painting her room, or picking out a gift for someone special. If you never wait in line because you ordered ahead or printed out boarding passes, priority game tickets, and reserved parking spaces, then you will find that your child won't appreciate having to stand in the line for the water fountain or patiently wait his turn for anything.

When you are willing to cook together and clean the house together, you are teaching your child important skills. He can one day become an expert cookie baker, furniture duster, or leaf raker. Of course, the most important thing you give him is the one thing he wants more than anything else: time with you.

The exchanges you have when you go to the library or the dry cleaners and those quick conversations with checkers at the grocery store—they all serve as lessons for your child. She will learn by watching and listening to you. She will learn how to treat people with whom she does not have a personal relationship. She will see that you are cordial and respectful but you are not best friends. She will begin to understand her own relationship with the people around her.

Chapter 4

School Life of Three- to Five-Year-Olds

THE SHOULDS

When your children are in preschool and the early elementary grades, you will be inundated by the *shoulds*. There are hundreds, maybe thousands, of lists out there telling you what your children should be doing when they are three and four or six and seven. Experts might warn that, in order for your little boy to be "ready" for kindergarten, he should be able to say his ABCs and recite his home address. Teachers might report that, because Susie can't write her name within the lines, she isn't "ready" for first grade.

You will need to be very careful when faced with the lists of tasks your children *must* master before they are ready for whatever comes next. In any given preschool or primary grade classroom, there are children who are developmentally one year ahead of their peers, and consequently, there are children who are a year behind their peers in their development. There are also lots of children in between. Developmental milestones are not met universally or predictably. What is predictable is that *most* children will meet *most* of the developmental milestones identified for a six-year-old by the time they are seven. Rather than losing sleep at night about your child lagging behind her peers, it will help to consider a few factors that contribute to this process.

Some little girls will play Star Wars, wrestle a toy away, and kick a soccer ball just like little boys. Others seem to stand out early because they are adept at organizing their environment and orchestrating activities and games for their playmates. They can seem smarter than the boys, and they are often more assertive than the boys. These little girls get everyone involved in a game of "house" or "family" in no time, taking the starring role of mother for themselves while satisfactorily directing everyone else in their minor roles.

Powerhouse girls and boys take charge, using their strong language skills to keep everyone on task. In preschool classrooms, they are often considered the teachers' helpers. There is no one bossier than a verbal three-year-old!

While boys might be focused on climbing and running and "fighting bad guys," their female friends might be learning to evaluate their situation and advocate for themselves. Most primary and preschool classrooms are language based. This provides a nice advantage for outgoing girls and very verbal boys. Don't worry, though; the girls and boys who are focused on learning how to shoot baskets or kick the soccer ball will catch up. They'll do it in their own time and when their brains and bodies are ready.

LEARNING HOW TO "BE IN SCHOOL"

Children in preschool and the elementary grades spend a good deal of time learning how to "be in school." Until they can learn how to follow the routines of the classroom, cooperate, listen to and follow instructions, get in line, take turns, and attend to the material, they are unlikely to be able to master the academic objectives.

Transitions can be particularly tricky for younger children. They are often loath to give up on an activity or project in which they have immersed themselves and will ignore or complain when the class has to move on. Leaving the playground can be particularly difficult for younger children, and the process requires calm determination and lots of patience on the part of teachers.

Children enter school at all stages of readiness. A younger sibling who has been hearing about school for a while might be anxious to see what all the excitement is about. He has been "practicing homework" or playing school with his siblings and is ready and raring to go. Another child might be more reluctant because she prefers the quiet company of her mother and long, lazy days at home. She might not be so comfortable with the unpredictability that comes along with being in a room with ten other children.

A child who has been raised in a language-rich home, where stories are read and told with great frequency, will look forward to diving into the classroom library, while a child whose family speaks English as a second language may be frightened by the pace and volume of her classmates' verbal exchanges. In a classroom of ten, there are ten very different little people with ten very diverse backgrounds and ten levels of readiness for school. With a talented teacher at the helm, a wide range of activities, lots of opportunities for play and interaction, and the passage of time, the children will form a cohesive group of active learners who enjoy their teacher, their classmates, and their school experience.

Amelia

Amelia was a beautiful little girl, the daughter of two parents and the little sister of Seamus, who was in second grade. Seamus was a confident boy, and he loved school. He was looking forward to welcoming his little sister to his school, where she would be in the pre-K class for four-year-olds. He spent lots of time that summer telling her about school, naming the teachers and students, and even showing her the yearbook so that she could see pictures of her teachers.

In July, Amelia stopped speaking completely. Her parents took her to the pediatrician, and he referred her for a battery of tests. There was nothing physically wrong with Amelia. The diagnosis was selective mutism secondary to anxiety. Amelia's parents were devastated. How could they send her to school if she could not or would not speak? Seamus had a somewhat different perspective on the situation. He suggested that, once she got to his school, where he felt safe and seen, that she would become comfortable, and she would begin to talk again.

After long conversations with school administrators and the teacher, Amelia's parents agreed to send her to school. The teacher assured them that she would keep a special eye out for Amelia and let them know if she seemed particularly upset or anxious. No one at school made a big deal about Amelia talking. The teacher told the other children, "Although Amelia is capable of speaking, she just isn't ready to talk yet, but we will wait to hear what she has to say when she's ready."

Amelia began talking again in October, albeit quietly and infrequently. Throughout her years at the school, Amelia was a quiet girl. She had friends, and she was an excellent student and a very good athlete. When it came time to go to high school, Amelia entered a large coed school. In the fall, she tried out for and made the soccer team.

Her teammates elected her to be their team captain. They admired her quiet consistency. They admired her lack of drama. They admired her relentless work and her kindness. Amelia needed time, patience, and support as she adjusted to being in school. She needed her teachers and her parents to stay with her as she adjusted. Fortunately, they did just that because they recognized that every child develops according to her own timetable.

Family structure can be a predictor of a child's readiness for the demands of school. First and only children might not be used to waiting for much. They will have to learn to wait their turn and to share toys. Children who have younger siblings might be very good at helping their peers or their teacher, but they might not be interested in listening to directions, as they may view themselves as little adults rather than children. Children in big families have likely learned how to share and play with one another easily, but they may not be as comfortable with the idea of sitting quietly and working alone.

Jack

Jack's father received the call to visit the principal's office. Jack was in the four-year-old prekindergarten class, and he was pushing the other kids down when they got in front of him in line. Jack's parents were pretty sure he was going to be expelled and that this infraction would go on his permanent record. The rookie principal was totally oblivious to the fact that she was scaring them to death. Jack wasn't quite sure what was going on and had clearly forgotten why or when he pushed anyone. The truth is, he was a first child, and he was used to being first. All it took to address this problem was a little explaining, some practice, and some praise when he held back his need to lead the line.

The principal, by now a veteran, had to talk with Jack about his behavior again when he was in fourth grade. A few of his classmates were giving one of the other boys a tough time. Jack was not involved—and that was the problem. She let Jack know that she expected more from him. She expected him to hold his classmates to a higher standard, to speak up for the little guy, and to remind his classmates that "we don't treat people like that." Jack became a quiet leader, setting a good example for his classmates while continuing to have fourth-grade-boy fun.

There came a time when the principal needed Jack to go beyond what was expected of his other eighth-grade classmates. A new student came to school in eighth grade, an anxious, brilliant, and charming boy. His anxiety manifested itself in obsessive-compulsive behaviors, and he needed someone to help him click back into what needed to be done. Jack was the guy. He remained with his new friend, reminding him to keep moving when he got stuck on one step, going up and back down repeatedly. He waited while his friend checked that the tables were all straight in the classroom and then encouraged him to go to lunch. Jack made an art of keeping close but never smothering and never telling anyone what he was doing.

At the end of the year, when the principal spoke to Jack's parents about how well he had dealt with his responsibilities and how much it had helped his friend, they knew nothing about it. She knew then that Jack would grow up to be a very special man one day. Jack's parents let him grow up, stumble, and work it out. They let his teachers expect a lot from him and encouraged him to develop habits that allowed him to meet those expectations. Jack's parents modeled civility and respect for him, and they set the bar high.

Jack went to college after spending four years at a nationally recognized, academically rigorous Jesuit high school, where the lessons of becoming

"Men for Others" resonated with him. Things started out a little rough for Jack, but with patience and an understanding of his particular situation and needs, Jack's parents and teachers supported him as he navigated the world of school, friendships, and responsibilities.

SCATTERED AND UNEVEN DEVELOPMENT

The little boy who can dribble a soccer ball while most of his peers are still trying to kick it once without falling down may be lagging behind in language or social skills. The little girl who can write her name perfectly and read sight words without a pause may struggle to make friends because she is too shy to leave the teacher's side during recess. Each of these children is developing at his or her own pace. You will want to be observant and aware of your children's strengths and needs, but this is not the time to compare or to panic.

GETTING TO KNOW THE TEACHERS

Be sure you know what your child's preschool and primary grade teachers expect of him. Ask questions. Do they understand that children develop at their own pace, or do they have a rigid set of objectives that all children must meet? Is your child experiencing success in the classroom? Is he feeling frustrated or inadequate because he is expected to complete worksheets every day? What benchmarks does the teacher use for measuring progress in the classroom? If you can see the teacher's list of developmental tasks, you can do an evaluation of your own just by observing your child at home or while he's playing with a friend.

Children who push or shove or grab toys from others can be labeled by adults as *aggressive*. Most of the time, these children simply do not yet have the cognitive flexibility to adjust on a moment's notice to changes in circumstances. They simply cannot locate the words to use when they want something, or they don't understand what's happening. Given a little extra time, a brief explanation, or a simple diversion, she can be helped along. Repeated opportunities to transition well and patient encouragement will help a child to experience smooth transitions and positive changes in expectations.

FOCUSING ON THE PROCESS

Of course you want your child to be a successful student one day, and you want to make sure her preschool and elementary teachers are preparing her for the increased academic expectations ahead, but you also want to remain respectful of her internal developmental clock. When preschool and elementary teachers hold the expectation that children should read before second grade, something has gotten off track.

Parents (and teachers) who focus on the product they want rather than the needs of the child in front of them disregard or are unaware of the consequences of demanding a child meet expectations she is unequipped to meet. By insisting that a child be "challenged" academically regardless of readiness, parents and educators ramp up academic expectations far too early. There is considerable evidence that pushing children to read before their brains are ready to read can lead to all kinds of problems—dyslexia, resistance to learning, and more.

WHEN SOMETHING IS WRONG

When your child struggles to recognize sight words and cannot articulate the letter sounds, please back off. If he cannot write his name on those dotted lines, don't insist that he does. His brain and his fingers are not ready. Instead, make letter shapes in the sand or out of playdough. Eventually, write his name in playdough, and trace the letters in sand. Draw them with shaving cream or bubbles in the bathtub. Everything is more fun when it's messy.

Say the letter names and the letter sounds aloud to yourself but forget about quizzing him. Read to him and talk to him—a lot. You will soon see and hear that he is beginning to make a connection between letters, words, and even sentences. Eventually he will learn to write and recognize his name. One day he will read his first book—when he is ready—and what a day that will be!

If math concepts are increasingly difficult for your daughter to grasp, take her shopping with you. Show her how to add and subtract on a calculator with large keys. Have her add up the items as you buy them or have her count the number of items you buy or the number of steps it takes to cover the whole grocery store. Play some board games to develop counting, strategic, and problem-solving skills. Of course, playing board games also allows you and your children to be together in a relaxed, low-pressure situation (unless your family is crazy competitive, which is okay, too!).

If you are worried that your child is not developing as she should during these early years, ask a trusted professional. Start with the classroom teacher and your pediatrician. Be specific about what you are seeing and what you think you should see. Ask the teacher direct questions about how your child functions within the classroom.

Generally, there are three types of teachers in the preschool and primary grades. There are teachers who report every misbehavior to you, and there are teachers who are reluctant to say anything negative about your child to you. You want to find a teacher who sees your child's positive characteristics and at the same time points out areas where he needs more practice or more instruction. You want a teacher who will partner with you as you help your child develop the social and academic skills necessary for success in school.

If the teacher's responses and the doctor's advice don't seem to address the concerns you have, go elsewhere. Find someone you trust—your own parents or a school administrator. Ask them to observe your child and give you honest feedback. Give your child time and opportunity to develop the skills, and after time, if those skills don't appear, revisit the topic.

WATCHING OUT FOR LABELS

Early intervention is effective and preferable for children who have significant learning or developmental lags. However, slapping a label on a child early in his school career can affect the way he is viewed by teachers, and it can limit or alter his opportunities for years to come. It is not something to be done lightly or without considerable consultation. Just as Amelia needed time and patience and not a label, there are many other children in preschool who don't need or deserve labels or targeted intervention. Labeling a boy like Jack aggressive literally could have altered the course of his life.

The solution to a lag in language skills can be straightforward. Talk, talk, talk. Read stories, tell stories, and narrate activities as you do them. Narrate your driving directions on the way home. Ask your child which way she thinks you should go on your walk to the park. Comment on the houses you pass, and pick out favorites. Take a trip to the zoo, and talk about the animals you see. Then go to the library and pick out some books about her favorite ones.

Speech therapy during these early years can provide just the boost a child with articulation issues needs. When speech therapists are willing to share methods and strategies with you, you can incorporate them into your daily interactions with your child without creating a situation where your child begins to think there is something wrong with her.

You know your child. If he is not progressing in the area of speech or socialization or if he still struggles to follow simple instructions after spending time in a structured, kid-friendly classroom and after you have practiced skills with him at home, then you should ask for help from someone. A school administrator with years of experience can guide you. Physical and occupational therapists, counselors, and child psychiatrists can be a wonderful resource for parents when children are seriously affected by delays. They are also trained to look for deficits.

When you and your children become participants in the education system, you will be faced with considerable new challenges. As parents, you will need to be critical consumers—examining carefully the culture of your children's schools and the people you entrust with the education of your precious child. You will need to remember that the charts and predictions are generalized guidelines, and they are not particularly useful when it comes to individual children. Each child develops in his or her own way, at his or her own pace. It's your job to be with your children—maintaining a balance between informed guidance and respect for your child's unique process of growth. Not all of us are meant to be the same, right?

Chapter 5

Family Life of Five- to Nine-Year-Olds

Remember the day your baby took his first step? Soon after that, he stumbled all the way from the chair to you. He lurched from one step to the other. He fell down over and over, plopping down on his diaper-thick bottom with a surprised look on his face every time. Then he made it. He got from one place to another—all the way across the room! You clapped and hugged, celebrating this remarkable accomplishment that would open the world to him and keep you on the watch for a good long time.

You encouraged him and cheered him on, even though you knew there were falls, bumps on the head, and skinned knees in the future, because you knew how this would end. You knew that soon he would have his balance. He would learn to run and skip, and he would do it all with grace and coordination.

STUMBLES AND FALLS

What if you hadn't known how it would turn out? You might have picked him up from that very first hard fall and carried him. You might have felt so badly for him. If you didn't want him to cry again, you might have helped him avoid the falls by carrying him around—forever! Could you try to remember those first faltering steps and those falls and your belief that they were a necessary part of the process? Can you transfer that knowledge to the challenges your children face as they grow up?

Of course you can! You can continue to cheer and encourage your child to take the risks because you know that stumbles and falls are simply part of the process of growing up. You can talk to your child about the risks you take and have taken. You can tell her about being afraid, acknowledging your fears, and then deciding to go for it anyway. You can talk about the times it didn't work out so well, remembering the hard things, the survival of the hard things, and the confidence gained in the process.

Children deserve opportunities to accomplish hard tasks and overcome obstacles. They need to be allowed to figure things out because, if they figure it out, they will learn from it. When children face a problem, whether it be with a friend or in math class, they feel uncomfortable. That discomfort will lead them to do one of several things. They will either ask someone else to solve the problem for them; they might just give up and walk away; or they will dig in and work hard to solve it. Unless you're going to be content with your adult child living in your basement, counting on you to manage his life, you know which of these choices you want him to start making right now.

If we let them, children can become addicted to mastering difficult tasks. They actually will seek out challenges, face them, struggle and fail, and then keep trying. (Think about some of those video games they cannot put down!) If you devote yourself to keeping your child's world easy and his way smooth, you will rob him of the joy and pride that comes from battles hard won.

Your child needs you to be in charge until she's grown. She shouldn't be asked to dictate what she will eat, what she will wear, which phone she will have, when she can use it, and which chores she will do. But if she doesn't get her way and you always jump right in to fix things for her, if you insist on handling things for her—easing her way—you make yourself so essential that she will never get a chance to grow up!

PITCHING IN

At home, your child should begin to contribute more to the family. When you tell a seven-year-old that it is his job to take out the trash each evening after dinner, he will likely forget. He might even try to avoid the job. He certainly isn't going to do it exactly as you would in the beginning. He might spill some of the trash, and he might forget to put a clean bag in the trash can under the sink.

How did you learn how to take out the trash, clean up spills, and put a new bag in? You learned by doing, and in the process of doing, you made mistakes. Your child will learn the same way. You will show him more than once, and he will learn. You will need to be consistent and precise. Don't let your fear of his failure impel you to do every job for him. If you try to save him from the hard work, you will also keep him from experiencing the great feelings that come with earned success.

Nagging about the trash and mentioning it five times before he responds will drive you both nuts. Think *once*: "I need you to take the trash out now." *Now* is the keyword. Establish eye contact and maintain it. Don't waiver, and don't entertain delaying tactics. Once your child knows that this is real, simple, and expected, you will not need to be as involved.

This process doesn't need to be a fight. It needs to be a taught responsibility. With responsibilities met come privileges. Don't forget to acknowledge a job well and consistently done. No reward is necessary. Rewards and bribery defeat the purpose—development of a sense of contributing to the family unit. After she has accepted and performed her job regularly and well, you can acknowledge her good work and provide her with an incentive to continue to be responsible.

For example, you can offer, "You are doing a good job taking the trash out every evening, and I notice that you are keeping your room clean these days. These things tell me that you are becoming more mature and more responsible. I think we should consider changing your bedtime from 8:30 to 9:00. What do you think?" Or when she asks to walk to a friend's house, you can respond, "I can see that you are becoming more mature and responsible, so I think that should be fine. Please be careful, and always let me know if something comes up and you need me."

Once you and your children have established the habit of helping out, your child's contributions to the functioning of his home will become second nature.

STAYING STEADY

PARENT: In five minutes, we will need to finish playing and clean up. *Warnings can ease transitions. Your child may or may not know how long five minutes is. It's the warning that counts.*

PARENT, FIVE MINUTES LATER: Time to clean up your toys. *Don't ask. Don't demand. Just say it's time.*

TOMMY: But my show's still on! *Or "I was going to practice foul shots, go to the bathroom, get a drink, and so on." This could be a great diversionary tactic by a clever child.*

PARENT: Oh, don't worry about that show. It comes on every afternoon. *Or "As soon as you pick up the toys, I will pour you a nice cold cup of water"; "Finish picking up now, and you'll have a half hour to practice your shots after dinner"; "Just hold it until we get the toys picked up, then you can use the bathroom and wash up for dinner," and so on. There is no threat here—just calm delivery of information and affirmation from a clever parent.*

It is important that this exchange takes place in the same space. If you call to your child from the other room, it is much easier for him to ignore you or "misunderstand" you. Be sure that you are face-to-face and that you make eye contact with your child when you two have this exchange. If you want to offer to help at the beginning, that's a good idea; just don't get caught doing it all.

With school-aged children, we want to confirm that they have responsibilities, and we want to communicate the expectation that they will fulfill those responsibilities. We want to do all of that in less than ten minutes, and we want to speak slowly! Think about Mr. Rogers and the way he mesmerized children. His slow and low approach to speaking, the fact that he never raised his voice above that certain tone, and the lack of inflection in his voice kept children riveted. Children process speech far more slowly than adults hand it out.

They also don't need a long explanation for why they need to come to dinner or get in the car or set the table. They just need the basics—what, when, and how:

PARENT: Don't forget about your room. You will need to clean it before dinner.

TESS: I'll do it later. *By now we know that* later *actually can mean* never—*or next* week. *This is where she tests your mettle!*

PARENT: Dinner is in thirty minutes. You'll need to clean your room before dinner. *Bite your tongue—nothing else! Calm, cool, and collected.*

These conversations can take place three or four times a day—conversations about the responsibilities children have, homework, and more. If it is important to you that your child understands what you are saying, you communicate that by speaking to him directly and making sure he is listening. Your posture and your tone will convey that this is not a casual request but rather an important direction.

The key is to make it brief, succinct, and clear and to be consistent in your expectations. If today you give in and serve her dinner before she cleans her room, you cannot rightfully expect her to think you're serious when you tell her to clean her room tomorrow.

Please notice that there is not an "or else" anywhere in these exchanges. This is where the natural consequences kick in. If Tess hasn't finished cleaning her room when dinner is on the table, then her dinner will get cold. Some children will need to see a timer in order to judge the amount of time they have. Go ahead and buy one of those big timers that shows just how much time there is and indicates the passing time if you think that might work for your child.

JOB WELL DONE!

School-aged children can help with setting and clearing the table, taking out the trash, even folding laundry. You will just have to learn to tolerate the speed and the care with which they engage in these chores. It may take twice as long to get the table set, dishes might get dropped, and things will undoubtedly be spilled. The towels might not be folded as neatly as you like, and some things will need to be put on the dewrinkle cycle.

Bigger projects like raking leaves or cleaning the bathrooms can and should include school-aged children. Boys who help clean the bathroom once a week may realize that, if their aim is better, they won't have so much to clean up. The time spent side by side raking leaves, washing the car, or weeding the garden is valuable time.

Conversations about school, friends, or dreams for the future take place naturally and comfortably when your children's hands are busy, and you and they aren't staring one another down across a table. The silence shared during those times can also help your particularly chatty and active children to come to appreciate the quiet.

Remind yourself that your children are *learning* to do things properly, and try to find something to celebrate each time they make a good attempt. Your approval matters. They will continue to try.

SIBLINGS

When you have precious little time to spend together as a family on a weeknight after long days at work and school and practices and homework and your children seem determined to fill that time with bickering and complaining, they are trying to tell you something important. Knowing that behavior is a form of communication, ask yourself, "What is behind this? What is that boy trying to tell me?" When you reframe the situation in your own mind, you will be far less likely to lose it and send him off to his room and far more likely to save the evening.

Take two minutes to quietly and calmly find out if there is something you can do to help him be able to participate in dinner and conversation. It is worth it. It might work with your daughter if you ask her if she's upset about something, but it might not work with your son. He could have a harder time identifying and articulating the feelings that are prompting his behavior. Best to identify the behavior, interpret it, and ask what you can do to help him regulate himself.

For example, you could say, "You are having a tough time working with your brother on cleaning up the Legos so that you can both join us for dinner. You seem really frustrated. What can we do together that will help you handle this?" It might be that he chooses to clean up the Legos alone because his brother's proximity is just getting on his last nerve. It might be that he puts away the other toys while his brother finishes the Legos. He can probably come up with something concrete once he realizes that you are not angry with him and that you want to help him extricate himself from this contentious situation.

SIBLING RIVALRY

It can be difficult not to interfere in arguments or struggles between your children. If you consider closely, you might notice that you view one sibling as in more need of your help while he deals with his articulate, clever sibling. While it's never a good idea to let one sibling take advantage of another, letting most things take their course will allow kids to understand one another better and keeps them on fairly even footing.

The one hard and fast rule should be that big kids don't get to hurt little kids physically or emotionally—at least not without hearing about it. That doesn't mean that older children don't get to tease or even take advantage of their younger siblings sometimes. Teasing or taking advantage might cause a younger child to become angry or frustrated, but as long as that's the extent of it, it is not cruelty. The older sibling will learn to regulate her behavior eventually, and the younger child has good "in-home" practice controlling his feelings. He may even figure out a way to make his older sibling pay for the teasing!

This is a natural process, and as children get older, it all evens out if they are given a chance to figure it out together. A little benign neglect can go a long way in your own family room. "Work it out" should be the first reaction. If you jump with both feet into every disagreement, you will communicate that your children cannot trust themselves or one another to resolve disputes. Your interference can get in the way of their bond. If a child can whine and cry every time her siblings want her to give in or to cooperate, they will eventually stop playing with her. However, expecting your older children to give in every once in a while to keep the peace allows them to experience a sense of maturity and an understanding that dealing with a toddler who hasn't learned how to cooperate yet requires a good deal of patience. Older siblings become aligned with the adults in the family and can adopt an attitude of loving acceptance.

As her three-year-old began to whine in a very high-pitched voice, "I waaaant thaaaat!" a young mother looked at her six-year-old son and said, "Please give her whatever it is that will stop her from making that noise." He smiled a little and nodded, then handed over the toy. He had helped his mom to "stop that noise," and he felt good that she had sought his help.

Children gain valuable skills from dealing with their siblings—negotiating, standing their ground, ignoring, and even competing. They will need these skills in school, on teams, and on the playground.

WHEN TO JUMP IN

One of the most important and hardest things for many parents to do is to hold back for a while if they think that something that is happening to their kids is unjust or if they think someone is judging their children too harshly or expecting too much. In these situations, if you can keep quiet and wait, most of the time things will work themselves out, or your child will figure out a way to handle the situation. This is hard to do and hard for kids to tolerate, but it usually pays off. If you bite your tongue, stop trying to fix every mess right away, and give your children a chance to create solutions to some of the problems they face, they will begin to see themselves as capable of meeting all challenges, and they will persevere. They may not enjoy hearing, "You'll be fine," but they will soon discover that they are.

Jasmine

Jasmine and her mother were butting heads a lot. Jasmine felt overlooked and sometimes took it out on her younger sisters. She could get pretty sassy with her mother, and she often refused to do what she was told. One morning, when she was particularly busy, Jasmine's mother showed her how to unload the dishwasher and where to put all the dishes and the silverware. The next morning, Jasmine got up early and joined her mother in the kitchen. She went to the dishwasher, opened it, and unloaded it, putting everything away where it belonged. She repeated this practice every morning after that.

In those early mornings, before her siblings were up, Jasmine had a chance to talk to her mother about the day ahead and tell her about things happening at school. She reconnected with her mother. Her mom was the person Jasmine most wanted to be with. Her behavior improved dramatically. She stopped sassing her mother, and when they made eye contact after a younger sibling had done something silly, they shared a knowing smile.

MAKING TIME FOR FREE TIME

There is a good deal of pressure these days that centers around organized activities for children. Parents may feel compelled to get their children on the "best" soccer teams or into the elite dance school. Many worry that their children won't get an opportunity to play a sport in high school or be a member of the traveling jazz band or get the starring role in the high school plays unless they enlist all kinds of coaches to teach them what they need to know to become all those things they want them to be. Some even have visions of college scholarships and the WNBA or the NHL. It is easy to lose track of the process by getting caught up in the product sought.

For your child's sake, try focusing on helping her work really hard at being a third-grader and playing really hard on one team or in one band. Encourage him to take advantage of some time every day to go outside and play without you hovering over him.

If you are schedule oriented and if you haven't yet given up on your dreams of an NBA star or a performance on Broadway, it will be hard for you to let your child wander. As your daughter strolls around the backyard picking dandelions, you might feel your blood pressure rising. As you watch your son build with Legos for hours, you might wonder if your vision of a future doctor might need to change to that of a future engineer. You might even feel the need to start exploring engineering camps.

Choice is the key. Children need to be allowed to develop their interests by trying out different personas and experimenting with different toys. They need to be allowed to be themselves at whatever point in their life, without the adults who surround them swooping in to either define them by or prohibit their interests in some way.

Children know the difference between play that is directed by someone else and self-directed play. They know when they are deciding how and what to play, and they are very aware when an adult is making those choices for them. They will learn far more when they make their own choices about whom to play with, what to play, and how to play.

Sally may like to bang on a pink piano today, but her parents may want to hold off on hiring the piano teacher because next week she may be far more interested in kicking the soccer ball. Mickey may like playing Barbies with his sister today and want nothing to do with them tomorrow. Kids play as a way of exploring the world around them and exploring their own personhood.

When you put too much stock in your child's curiosities or temporary interests, you risk ruining it for your child. Young people will become who they will be as long as you love who they are right now and let them have time and the opportunity to become. Try to remember that you are all—children and parents—in the middle of the process! Children need to wander, and they need to direct their own play sometimes, with no other purpose than wandering and playing. Find a good book to read, or do a little wandering yourself, but let them do the business of being children.

BOYS WHO WRESTLE AND SMELL FUNNY

When boys are in elementary school, their behaviors can sometimes push their mothers—and often their fathers—to come close to losing their minds. If she loses her temper with them, they rarely hold it against her for very long. They'll let her steal a kiss or a hug, and then they move on to more important things.

In many boy-oriented houses, lamps get broken by errant basketballs, and doorknobs and chair backs are perpetually sticky. There is very little drama in a boy house, and the tears that fall are genuine. They are usually brought on by bumps, bruises, and broken bones; a spat with a sibling; or a scolding from a parent. But lots of women have a hard time with their boys. They struggle to understand the "why" behind boy behavior. They want to coddle and cuddle them, and they want to protect them from fighting for something important to them. *Important* is the keyword here. What is very important to boys often seems trivial to their mothers. When a boy comes home from school frustrated because the teacher took away the soccer ball at recess when the boys were arguing or when he gets sent to the principal's office for defending his friend who is being bullied, his mom is likely to jump in and want to protect him from his misery. Her first instinct might be a phone call to the school. If, however, she lets him talk about how unfair the ball policy is and if she helps him to consider alternative approaches to bullying, then she acknowledges his need to stand up for himself and others. Maybe he can figure out a way to talk to the teacher about how important it is for the boys to play soccer during recess, and maybe he and his friend can approach the bullies in a way that doesn't include physical confrontations or trips to the principal's office.

What looks like craziness to women doesn't seem the least bit odd to boys. Boys can look right at their mothers and never recognize the "angry mom" face. Consequently, when they receive a scolding for misbehavior, they are usually taken by surprise, and they are hurt because they truly thought that their mothers were enjoying their antics.

Their favorite things to do at a six-year-old birthday party might be to wrestle and see who can roll down the hill the fastest. Of course, they do all of that after inhaling two hot dogs, two pieces of cake, a scoop of ice cream, and five glasses of lemonade each. Boys throw up a lot more than girls do, and almost none of it is due to stomach viruses. They get bloody noses far more often, too. You can attribute that to very aggressive nose picking or because they wrestle and roll so much.

But boys also can be funny, soft-hearted, physical, genuine, and resilient. They still want and need love and affection from their parents, and they are desperate to learn everything they can about the world and their place in the world. Your example will show them how to be gentle and strong, adventurous, and wise.

Boys in the middle grades can be awkward, sometimes smelly, and always curious and desperate to learn. They still want you to read to them, and they still want you to tuck them in. They have fragile souls and egos, and they deserve to be treated gently.

GIRLS' SELF-IMAGE

Many girls in the middle grades focus much of their attention on the adults around them. They want to please their teachers and the important adults in their lives. They are idealistic and sometimes perfectionistic. If your daughter expresses consistent concerns about the way she looks, if she uses labels like "fat," "ugly," or "disgusting" to describe herself or others, then you have some work ahead of you. If she has somehow been convinced that she is ugly, either by in-person or cyberbullies, you need to address that. If she is simply struggling with the fact that she has not yet begun to develop physically or that she has developed too soon for her liking, you still need to know and do something about it.

Make sure that you and your daughter talk about the physical changes that take place during early puberty. Use diagrams, pictures, and books that your daughter can look over when she wants to. Many girls start to see those changes when they are as young as seven or eight, and they are unprepared for them. Knowledge is power, and if you and your daughter can talk about what's happening now, what's ahead, and why it all happens, she will be far less fearful. She might even be a little curious and a tad excited.

This is a good time for a first mother-daughter discussion about how those early years were for her, before she became a young woman. This is also the time to encourage your daughter to play. She should be able to find a sport that interests her. If not, then make a date with her for a daily walk and talk with her. She will treasure the closeness that you are offering. She will establish a practice of healthy exercise, and it will give her an opportunity to talk with you about her life, her dreams, and her struggles.

The natural pudginess that often precedes and accompanies physical development in girls will not get out of control if she is exercising and eating right. Beware, though! There is a difference between talking about and living a healthy lifestyle and discussing weight issues with a girl of eight. Unless your daughter is obese, her body size and shape before puberty will have little to do with her body size and shape when she is an adult or even a teen. The only thing you will accomplish with weight control conversations at this point are damage to her self-image and the beginnings of an obsession with weight. Eating disorders among young girls are not unheard of, and they can be life altering, if not deadly.

In this new world that is opening up to your daughter, she will take the early steps toward creating a vision of herself based on her relationships with you, her teachers, her coaches, and her peers. You will want to provide plenty of opportunities for your daughter to talk to you about what she is experiencing and how that vision is beginning to look.

It's important for daughters to spend time with their fathers doing yard work, reading, shooting baskets, and building things, so that she will see herself as competent in areas that are often restricted to boys. Camping trips and trips to the grocery store will allow her to see her father as both a resource and a champion. Dads can teach their daughters some very powerful and useful lessons.

She should learn to whistle really loudly from her parents. She might need that whistle someday. She can learn that it's good to laugh at herself and that taking herself too seriously can be exhausting. Parents can encourage their daughters to speak up when something is not right. They can talk about women they know who do that and how much they admire them.

Using a screwdriver, hammering a nail, and changing a tire on her bike are skills girls (and boys) can learn from their father. Later he can teach her how to change a tire on the car. Most importantly, a daughter's dad can teach her that her smile is a gift to the world and that she should share that gift whenever and wherever she can.

PREPARATION

No one enjoys being caught off-guard. Everyone wonders what to expect in new situations, and children are no different. They can learn how to act in different settings, and they best learn these things experientially. For example, taking children to church services without preparing them ahead of time is unfair to the children and other attendees. Ahead of time, young children need to know what is expected of them for the next forty-five minutes to an hour, and they need to hear about those expectations each and every time you attend services. Afterward, you will want to be specific about what your child did well and what she needs to keep working on. If a child is finding it hard to whisper, then practice whispering for a little while every day. This can be fun and funny.

If a child has trouble sitting still, you can help him learn what it feels like to keep his body still. Practice sitting and standing still at home—be statues or soldiers or play Simon Says and Red Light, Green Light. Children will learn to transfer these skills to the appropriate settings if we give them time to practice them and provide them with specific feedback after they try them out at church or at the library. Finally, a quick and quiet update on how much time is left in the service is helpful. Letting your child know that you are halfway through or that the end is coming up very soon will help with the restlessness that she naturally feels.

Maybe you've always envisioned a wonderful trip to the theater with your children—complete with dressy clothes, a ride on the metro, and center orchestra seats. You buy the ridiculously expensive tickets. You dress yourselves up, and off you go. Ten minutes into the performance, Susie wants to go to the bathroom. Twenty minutes in, Johnny wants to know when it's over. By intermission, everyone really needs a snack. Hopefully the $5.00 water and the $10.00 cookies will carry them through.

The second half of the performance finds your children squirming and wondering, "When can we go home?" When it's finally time to go home, as you travel from the theater, you feel so disappointed. This didn't turn out the way you envisioned it at all! There are lessons to be learned here—by the adult.

Next time, you will know. You will know that you need to read the story to your children several times before you go to the play so that they know what's happening on the stage. Next time, everyone will go to the bathroom before the play starts. Next time, everyone will whisper if they have questions. Next time, you will show them how to use the playbill so that they know what's coming up and how many scenes there are before and after intermission.

Next time, everyone will go to the bathroom again during intermission. Next time, you will not ask very young children to fulfill your dreams of a day at the theater. Finally, you will look around and find a children's theater so that your children can practice watching a play before you spend another fortune at the Kennedy Center.

UNCOMPLICATED DISCIPLINE

The boundaries between adults and children exist to protect children. Adults who respect those boundaries set expectations for behavior and communicate those expectations clearly. As long as the expectations are aligned with the developmental needs and tasks of their age, children will do their best to meet them. They will, of course, sometimes miss the mark, but that is part of growing up.

There are some routines that are essential to the successful operation of the family: for example, quiet time on weeknights so that children can complete homework and parents can provide support for homework, meals together without devices, Saturday morning chores, and so on. Family rules that include eating healthy meals and parents monitoring internet, social media, and television programs all allow for predictability and consistency. These practices make it possible for the family to operate smoothly and relatively efficiently.

Privilege and Responsibility

Privileges and responsibilities are constantly changing in families. As children get older or when they demonstrate an inability to follow the rules, the rules must be adjusted to meet their needs and the needs of the family as a whole.

Clear Parameters

A seven-year-old can play in the fenced yard without an adult supervising, and he needs to check in with his mom or dad if he wants to go down the street with a friend. He can play his video game for a specific amount of time, and he will clean up his toys after playing. Parameters like these should be clear to everyone, and when they are followed, the family can function smoothly. They are concrete and specific and therefore relatively easy for children to grasp and follow.

When positive family relationships are a priority, children and parents treat one another respectfully. Children and adults do not scream at one another; they tell the truth; they do not gossip; they choose to be kind rather than cruel; and they look out for one another. While these concepts may be a little harder for children to grasp, they are based on family values, and they are reflected in specific behaviors, so they eventually come naturally to children and adults.

Balancing Expectations and Reality

Of course, your children must be able to do what you are asking them to do. For example, a five-year-old can sit still at the dinner table until everyone is finished, but a three-year-old may need something to entertain him during that time. "Clean your room" may not be a clear enough direction for a small child. She may need step-by-step directions, but as she gets older, she needs less oversight. As children develop, they need to be given reasonable responsibilities within the family. A six-year-old can learn to make her bed neatly and put her toys away.

It can be difficult to balance family expectations with reality. Outside obligations like practice, work, homework, and playtime can seem destined to sabotage your plans at every turn. This is where realistic flexibility kicks in. Keeping in mind that sometimes the trash waits a day to go out because there are other obligations to be met can allow everyone to take a breath and avoid panic. Getting back on schedule will just require a little creativity and patience. Then you can return to your system of regular instruction, endless patience, and a willingness to wait and watch. None of these concepts are very prevalent in a world where we can usually get anything we want done immediately. These disruptions in what seemed like the perfect plan can give you a run for your money. The difficulties presented by uncontrollable factors can help you to remember that, while you aim for the perfect, you know things can't be perfect all the time.

Children thrive when you show them what excellence looks like and encourage them to strive for it. Excellent behavior and excellent work can become a habit. A homework paper that is written illegibly is not acceptable because it is not representative of the good mind, the standards, and the innate ability of the child who hands it in. Tempting as it might be, you won't want to redo the assignment for your child.

If you expect your children to stand up when an adult comes into the room or to hold the door for others *every single time*, they will. If you remind them to look people in the eye and speak clearly, they will. Consistent high expectations and lots of practice help children to develop habits of excellence.

When expectations are realistic, consistent, and reasonably adjusted as they grow up, children will establish patterns of good behavior and see themselves as contributing and valued members of the family. You may veer off-track periodically—expecting too much or too little—but you can always adjust to the child and the situation.

Make sure your children understand that you know they are better than any one mistake or any one error in judgment. Let them know that you appreciate their efforts, and celebrate their successes with them. They will do their best to live up to your standards. The key is to balance accountability, respect for self and others, knowledge of your child's capabilities, gentleness, and the understanding that no one does things perfectly every time.

NONPUNITIVE DISCIPLINE

Discipline is often misunderstood. Many people think that to discipline a child is to punish the child for breaking a rule. The trouble is, if you are only reacting—punishing something already done—you fail to teach the child to try something different when the same or similar situation arises again. Punishment and isolation only serve to disconnect a child from the community in which he is trying to learn how to live, and they further separate him from you—the one person to whom he must be connected.

The goal of discipline is to help children to develop self-discipline in their daily habits. So make sure your children understand that your behavioral expectations are based on the fundamental premise that all people are called to love and respect one another and that their safety is a priority. You demonstrate your belief in this premise by treating your children and everyone else with love and respect. Eventually, they learn to examine their own behaviors, adjust them if needed, and establish positive habits. You cannot expect your beloved children, brilliant and capable as they are, to do things right the first time. Patience and persistence are the keys.

MISTAKES

No one can develop appropriate social skills all by himself. He needs other people for that! So effective discipline includes accountability for actions, of course, but it's more than that. Recognizing that children will make mistakes either because they don't know what to do or because they choose to do something that they know is wrong, parents can create opportunities for their children to make things right. You cannot possibly anticipate every behavior gone wrong that might occur, so sometimes instruction about acceptable behaviors has to come after the fact.

The little girl who cuts a hole in her new jeans because she is struggling to scratch an itchy mosquito bite on her leg will obviously need instruction after the fact (before she destroys any more clothes!). She will need to be taught that there are other ways to reach the itch that will allow her to be able to wear those jeans again.

Then there is the instruction that needs a little more clarification. The little boy who draws on the wall in his room with a marker is told, "We never draw with markers on the wall." He is sufficiently sorry, and after cleaning the wall, his mom feels confident that he will not repeat the behavior. Soon thereafter, she comes upstairs to see that he has drawn on his dresser with a marker. She is stunned and may lose her temper a bit as she asks him why he would do such a thing. He responds tearfully, "I thought it was only the wall." If only Mom had said, "We only use markers on the construction paper we keep in the desk downstairs."

POOR BEHAVIOR

When parents are in agreement regarding expected behavior at home, it is much easier to keep things under control. However, when one parent is too occupied or too tired and decides to ignore certain behaviors, the implication is that she supports the behavior. This is how children become confused about whether they are expected to follow all the rules all the time. Letting it slide is sometimes the easy way out, but it's not so good for children. Of course, not everything is worth a fight when it comes to children's behavior, but some things are. The adults in the family need to decide together and ahead of time where they can give a little and what is absolute.

Parents are stretched. There are so many demands on your lives. When children refuse to take no for an answer, when they beg and beg and beg for whatever it is that they want, even when they have been told no multiple times, they have some sense that eventually you will give in. That's because they've had success with this strategy before. Exhausted, you might give in, especially when you have an audience—in the grocery store, at a friend's house, whenever others are watching.

Just because you've made this mistake once or even if you've made it fifty times, it doesn't mean you can't start today explaining to your child, "From now on, when I tell you that you cannot have something, I do not want you to keep asking me. I have made the mistake of giving in in the past, but I will not do that anymore." Then, you have to stick to it, ignoring the fifty "Pleases," the stomping feet, and the tears until your child understands that they no longer work. You might even get an "I hate you" or two, but stay with it, and eventually your child will understand that the rules have changed.

Consider the child who doesn't follow the rules, even when you feel confident that she has learned them. She may be able to repeat the rules, but does she understand how to follow them? She may not understand that rules are transferable to slightly different circumstances. She might be unable to follow the rule because she's too young, too tired, too hungry, or needs your attention. She may be certain that you won't follow through when she chooses not to follow the rules.

Depending on the misbehavior, there are consequences, even if they are unintended—natural consequences. If your third-grader doesn't study for her spelling test, then she might get an F. If she spends all evening watching television or playing games, then she will likely face a teacher who wants homework assignments turned in in the morning. Then, if her mother finds out, she will lose her television and gaming privileges.

If your six-year-old insists on finishing his game when he is supposed to come to dinner, then he will miss dinner and be hungry in a couple of hours. You're going to feel mean when you enforce the consequence of missing dinner, but you'll only have to do that once or twice. He will survive without dinner. Later, when you tell him how much you missed seeing and talking with him at dinnertime, he will understand that you want him to join the family for dinner, and he will learn to postpone his game and come when he's called.

You want to make it clear to your children what you expect, but always remember that the more rules you have, the more opportunities there are to break the rules. While your values remain the same, your tactics might work beautifully with one child and fail miserably with another. Rules and consequences need to evolve as your children get older. What works for a nine-year-old is inappropriate for his fifteen-year-old sister. When your first child follows your "don't go in the street" rule the first time and every time, you can almost count on your second child to challenge the rule at every opportunity.

AN ATTITUDE OF OPTIMISM

During these early years, adults and children are finding their way. Discovery, curiosity, flexibility, and a willingness to take the time are essential. You are creating a safe and solid foundation on which you can continue the process of growing your children.

Children want to please their parents and teachers. They believe what important adults say about them. When you praise his efforts, he will work harder. When you hold the bar high, he will do everything he can to reach it. Children watch what you do, and they listen to what you say to them and to the people around you. They are absorbing your life philosophy, whether you want them to or not.

If you spend your days complaining about work, coworkers, or your kids and all they need, your children will take those complaints to heart. If, though, you can find something to laugh about and bring yourself to accept that some days just don't go the way you want them to, then you will model important life lessons for your children. Let them hear about what you did well that day and your failures. Laugh at yourself and your predicaments. Explain what you plan to do to handle things differently tomorrow, and express confidence in your ability to make things come out right.

If you can approach each day with a clearly communicated sense of gratitude—for the beautiful sunshine or a colorful garden—if you can communicate an honest optimism as you look ahead to a task, your children will adopt qualities of gratitude and optimism. If you can laugh at yourself and your circumstances and you make a conscious effort to express joy, your children will see life as fun and full of joy.

They will come to understand that difficulties—in tasks and with other people—are to be expected, but those difficulties do not define the quality of life and work. Your children will see that struggles and obstacles are just bumps in the road, nothing more and nothing less. They will begin to grasp that they can avoid some bumps, and others will require their best efforts to manage. They will also see that you don't allow any of those bumps, even when there are a lot of them, to ruin the trip because you make sure that you find the good stuff in every day.

FOCUSING ON THE GLITTER

Let's face it, each child brings great joy, and each breaks your heart just a little at one time or another. If you can move your focus away from, "I want my son to be . . . " or "All I want for my daughter is . . . ," then you can come back to the work you are called to do today. You can share the glittery moments: the sound of your children laughing in the next room, her crystal-line voice as she sings to the radio, the bedtime hug, and the weight and warmth that sets in as he leans back to hear one more story. You and your children can develop an appreciation for the gifts they have been given, and an understanding that their mission in life is not to be happy or satisfied but rather to appreciate and make good use of those gifts.

The idea that each child is known and loved and each is given a specific mission to discover and fulfill is a powerful one. You can take advantage of the ordinary events and simple moments to make sure your children know they are loved unconditionally by communicating your belief that they are capable of great kindness and compassion. You can teach them to notice the opportunities—to notice someone in need or the beauty of the world or when someone needs a friend.

If together you laugh at your predicaments and you resolve to keep going when your burdens seem heavy, together you will move forward. If you acknowledge your mistakes, if you say sorry when it's called for and thank one another for being there, then you become stronger as individuals and as families.

Chapter 6

Social Life for Five- to Nine-Year-Olds

As children enter the primary grades, they continue to develop the social and emotional skills they will need to get along in the world. They identify best friends, and they become aware that there are children they don't particularly like to play with. Boys and girls play together, and their games tend to involve lots of running, grabbing, and plotting captures.

Children begin to accept that their own perspective is not the only perspective. They disagree with others, and sometimes they have to give in. They begin to manage their emotions, and they start to take responsibility for their schoolwork and their self-care.

MAKING FRIENDS

During these early years in school, children begin to establish friendships with their classmates or teammates, and those friendships usually arise based on common interests. They will be invited to playdates at a friend's house, birthday parties at the bowling alley, and even sleepovers. It is your job to decide what works for your child and your family while considering your child's need to establish positive relationships with friends.

If you're a working parent, the last thing you might want to do is give up a Saturday afternoon with your son so that he can go to a friend's house or a birthday party. You might feel guilty, though, if you decline the invitation. Invitations can be accepted in moderation. You could limit it to maybe only two hours at the friend's house, and maybe you can go with him to the birthday party at the bowling alley. You don't have to participate, but you can be there, and you can get a glimpse of how he operates in his world.

There is nothing wrong with limiting the amount of time your elementary school–aged child spends at other people's homes and conversely limiting the amount of time friends spend in your home. Your first priority should always be the needs of your family. It's not your goal to make friends with other parents. Your second-grader might be disappointed if he misses a birthday party every once in a while, but if he's spending his time with you at a park, in the backyard throwing catch, or in the kitchen making cookies, then he will be glad you made the choice.

When they spend time at friends' houses, children get a glimpse of the ways that different families operate. Maybe the parents pretty much let them do what they want while they are there. Maybe the mom cooks a hot lunch, and everyone sits down to eat together. Maybe the dad is a little scary, or maybe he's a little funny. Maybe their house is neat as a pin, with toys put away immediately after playing, or maybe there is stuff scattered everywhere.

SLEEPOVERS

Kids love sleepovers. Mostly they love the idea of sleepovers—spending a long night without parental supervision, eating snacks, watching movies, playing games, staying up all night long—all these are very appealing to seven-year-olds.

Sleepovers can be messy for parents and kids. Allowing your seven-year-old to spend the night at a friend's house is a risk. First, there's a good chance she won't make it through the night, and you'll be driving over in your pajamas to pick her up. She may be perfectly fine staying with another family, but you might lie awake all night worrying about whether she's lonely or whether she'll wet the bed because she's afraid to get up in the night. Do you discourage your daughter from bringing her stuffed animal or favorite blanket? Will she be able to sleep if she doesn't have it?

What about in the morning? Remember when you stayed at a friend's house and you woke up first? You couldn't decide whether to get up and go downstairs or stay in bed until your buddy woke up. Or maybe you woke up to find that he was already downstairs! Then you had to make the lonely walk down to the kitchen by yourself, wondering how you would be received when you arrived.

The day after a sleepover is a lost day. Your child will be tired because he and his friend were up until all hours, and you will be frustrated because you let him go, and now he's tired and cranky.

Sleepovers provide children with a window into other families' lives, and they learn to see how much families can differ, but they should be few and far between. There are too many pitfalls, and too many things that can go wrong. Try letting your daughter stay at the friend's house until 9:00 or 10:00 at night, and then pick her up. Everyone will sleep better, and the next day will not be a total loss.

THE NEEDY FRIEND

In any elementary and middle grade class, there is usually a boy or girl who wants to have a friend over all the time. If your child is constantly invited to this child's house—to the point where you will park down the street to avoid running into him or his mother—you need to come up with a new tactic.

Maybe this child is a lonely only or youngest child, or maybe his parents are far more lenient when he has a friend over, or maybe he really wants to be best friends with your child, and he's afraid someone else might steal him away. Of course you feel bad for the lonely child, and you're a little flattered by the fact that your child is in high demand for playdates. You just don't want to be loaning your child out regularly because you like having him around, and you want to do things with him. A conversation with the child's parent is in order: "We are so glad that Billy and Joe have become friends, and we are appreciative of the many times you have invited Joe to your home. He has fun with Billy. We are finding, however, that we are not getting enough time with Joe these days, and we will be declining playdate invitations indefinitely. We would like to have Billy at our house periodically, though. Maybe he could come over next Saturday for a couple hours in the morning. We have an obligation in the afternoon, but if he'd like to come from 10:00 to 12:00, we would love to have him." In this way, you are putting an end to Joe's visits to their home, and you are opening your home to Billy, with limits.

BALANCING ACT

It can be a juggling act, balancing friendships, extracurriculars, and family time for young children. Your child still needs to know you want to be with him, and he still wants to spend time with you. Now, though, he also needs to expand his horizons a bit. It is important for your child to make friends and navigate the demands of friendships while balancing family, school, and social demands. She cannot manage this on her own. She will need your help.

ATHLETICS

In 1972, Title IX was signed into law as part of the Civil Rights Act. While positive changes took a while to really take hold, in the last twenty-five to thirty years, girls and young women have been welcomed into the world of school athletics. No longer are they expected to sit on the sidelines; rather they are encouraged to participate and compete fully.

Many children at this age are becoming more capable when it comes to athletics. They are more coordinated, faster, and stronger than they were just a year ago. They will likely begin to appreciate more the differences in athletic ability among their peers. They may even begin to point out how much better they are in sports than their peers. They may avoid playing with the boys or girls who are not quite as coordinated as they are and may do almost anything not to include those children on their teams.

Winning is usually very, very important to boys. Once they escape the restrictions of the average fourth-grade classroom, they are more than ready to engage in an intense soccer, football, or basketball game. If their classmate cannot keep up, they might get frustrated, and they might even tell that classmate that he can't play.

There are lots of lessons to be learned around sports, even recess sports. First, this is a good time to talk to your child about humility. He needs to know that other people will recognize his abilities, but they will never know or need to know how hard he has worked to develop those skills. He needs to know that, just because he is talented, it doesn't mean he is more valuable, more important, or more special than anyone else.

If your child has good skills, she should use them to play her hardest in every game, but she can also use them in off times to help her classmate who isn't quite so good learn to dribble or shoot.

What if your child refuses to try a new sport or gives up quickly when he cannot master a new skill easily? Some children are so concerned about disappointing or failing that they will only do what they are good at. It is important to acknowledge that it's always more fun to do what you know, and when you excel at something, it feels great. Then you can reintroduce the idea of working hard on something that doesn't come easily.

Pushing herself to learn a new skill and get really good at something that doesn't come naturally will allow your child to broaden her world and to experience firsthand what it feels like to persist despite challenges. When she wants to quit, really wants to quit, because it's not fun and it's too hard, make one suggestion. Suggest that your child take a page out of the long-distance runner's book: by telling herself to keep going, to try harder, to do better especially when it's hard to keep going. Imagine the incredible sense of accomplishment, the joy she will experience when she keeps at it and reaches the goal!

What about that boy who isn't quite as good as his classmate in sports or in the academic arena? He might be jealous of his friend, and he might find reasons and opportunities for saying cruel things to or about him. There can be a prevailing sense of competition in almost everything children this age do. It can be tough for a young boy to realize that he cannot beat out his best buddy no matter what he does. This is a good time to introduce the concept of "yet." He isn't as good in math or baseball as Mark is *yet*. He hasn't gotten all As on his report card like Mark has *yet*.

Reminding children in this age group that they are far from cooked, that there is a lot more that will happen before they are grown, will help with jealousy. Finding reasons to celebrate what your child can do is all the more important. The message is, "You are right where you are supposed to be right now. If you keep working hard, you will continue to make progress. You are more than enough right now."

If your daughter has been told by peers or coaches that she's just not good enough, then you will need to do some work on her self-confidence. You'll need to let her know that there is no need to worry about being as good as anyone else; rather she should worry about doing what it takes to get better than she is today. Talk about a time when someone else's evaluation of your skills made you wonder if you would ever be good enough. Talk about how great it felt to keep working and get better despite being discouraged by someone else's words.

The natural resentment your daughter might feel for those who do things better than she does needs to be dealt with. You can help her appreciate how good her friend is at soccer or football, remarking on the amazing goal the friend scored or the great pass she threw. There isn't a limited pool of talent out there, and just because your child's friend is really good doesn't mean your child can't, with hard work, get really good.

You've been there. A colleague you like is getting all the accolades, and you feel ignored or left out. You feel unappreciated and inadequate. Once you acknowledge the great job your colleague is doing and you congratulate him for doing such a good job, your jealousy takes a back seat to genuine appreciation and admiration.

SOCIAL HIERARCHIES

In fourth and fifth grade, girls and boys will begin to establish social hierarchies in their classrooms. These hierarchies are strengthened on the playground and at weekend sleepovers and birthday parties.

Most girls in fourth and fifth grade begin to care about the way they look and dress, and they begin to talk about one another. Most boys at this age are happily unaware of how they look. If your daughter does not care about what she wears or how her hair looks, if she doesn't engage in the complicated social exchanges that begin to emerge at this time, she will be fine as long as she has a friend or two with whom she can spend time. Your daughter may prefer to travel light, avoiding the larger cliques that girls form and limiting her activities to those she can do with one or two friends.

RELATIONAL BULLYING

Relational bullying used to be the purview of middle and high school. Now that students who are eight, nine, and ten have cell phones in their pockets and iPads in their bedrooms, relational bullying can threaten them—possibly even more than it does older children.

Relational bullying can begin for the smallest reason. Two children might have a minor disagreement, or one might imagine that she has been slighted by the other. She does not feel comfortable confronting her friend, so she just stops talking to her. Even when asked, she may refuse to say why she is angry. At least she refuses to tell the girl with whom she is angry. She does, though, tell her other friends. They tell other friends, and what was a minor snag in a friendship blows up to be a huge conflict.

The more mature girls and the girls who have older siblings are usually more savvy than their counterparts, and they might engage in relational bullying that, absent adult attention, can have long-lasting effects on their peers. Girls who are bullies, those who are victims, and those who are bystanders need extra adult supervision and direction at this time in their lives. Given opportunities to talk with trusted adults and with one another about what is happening to them, they can come to an understanding that relational bullying hurts all of them. This is where it can be helpful for your daughter to have a female teacher. Women are far too familiar with the subtleties of early relational bullying, and they can step in to put a stop to it before it goes too far.

CELL PHONES

Children as young as six are bringing cell phones to school, so parents have some serious catching up to do. There is no reason for a child this young to have a phone, unless he uses public transportation to get to and from school. If he brings his phone to school, what is he using it for? Is he texting other kids? Is he reporting his every move to his parents? Is he playing Candy Crush? Parents who think their children need a cell phone in case of emergency have forgotten that school personnel have access to telephones, and they can reach parents, police, firemen, and pretty much anyone they need to reach.

Children at this age do not have the sophisticated decision-making ability that allows them to reasonably consider before they post pictures of themselves or chime in on cyberbullying. They also don't have a well-developed self-image, so the cruelty that is so prevalent on social media can hit them particularly hard.

Girls whose bodies develop early can be taunted and teased, and they are more likely to be victims of sexual harassment by older boys online and in person. They might be asked to send pictures of themselves in revealing poses, and they may not realize the implications of doing so. Girls who are late to develop physically and girls who are particularly naive can fall prey to the cruelest comments about their looks and their naivete. Because they are still in the early stages of understanding what it means to be an adolescent girl, they are particularly vulnerable to believing that they are ugly, deformed, stupid, or fat.

BIG DREAMS AND QUIETING DOWN

Somewhere around fourth and fifth grade, when many boys begin to believe that they are destined for fame and fortune in the NFL or the NBA, girls might begin to question their own significance. They may experience success in the classroom but have trouble figuring out what the world expects of them because they are surrounded by images and messages that place little value on academics and an inordinate amount of value on social dominance.

This is the time to make yourself available on a consistent basis. Set aside time each week when you and your daughter can do something together. Rather than shopping for a new outfit, which could lead to disagreement, ask her to help you pick out new porch furniture or a new rug for her room. Just having the time with you might be enough to encourage a conversation about the complex social challenges that she might be facing. If you have avoided judgmental statements like "I cannot believe the way that child dresses!" or "She is way too aggressive when she plays soccer," then you might find your daughter wants to talk about just those kinds of things.

This is not the time to solve her dilemmas for her by telling her to avoid the girl who dresses provocatively or making sure that she's aggressive when she's in the game, no matter what anyone says. These kinds of statements will shut down the conversation quickly. Instead, ask her how she feels about being on the soccer team—what the positives *and* the difficulties are. It won't hurt to share your take on the benefits of sports participation for all kids.

She does want to know what you think, even if she doesn't say so. Ask her why she thinks some girls feel compelled to dress like they are much older. Ask her if that's enough to keep her from being friends with those girls. Not all of this can be covered in one trip to the furniture store. Consistent, reliable availability is the key. Listening to your girl and appreciating her insights and her thoughtfulness will give her opportunities to share a little of her world with you and to get your take on things about which she is confused.

CAMPS

Caution is the key when deciding if your child is ready for a sleepaway camp, particularly for girls. If the camp includes older girls, then there are all kinds of potential hazards ahead. Middle and high school girls often enjoy "adopting" certain younger girls and showering them with attention and far too much information about life as a teen. They even go so far as to dress them up and put makeup on them. Think about what type of camp this will be, and decide if it will foster your daughter's sense of confidence and her capabilities.

HOLDING YOUR OWN

When your child's life is increasingly busy, when school and activities seem to overshadow family time, it is important for you to designate certain times as sacred. Maybe it's dinner every night—no matter what else is happening. Maybe it's Friday night pizza and movies or Saturday morning trips to the big-box store. Make sure that you always reserve reading time before bed, and don't give that up for anything!

While it might be tempting or seem easier to step back and let teachers and other adults assume some of the responsibility for the education and guidance of your child, this is absolutely not the time to abdicate your parenting responsibilities. Instead, this is the time when you reinforce your values and the high expectations you hold in order to counter the cultural messages that will inevitably invade your child's life as she moves through the primary and middle grades.

Chapter 7

School Life of Five- to Nine-Year-Olds

Children are made to develop according to their own internal template. In any given classroom, there are children who are focusing all their efforts and energies on physical skills, while others are developing language and speech skills. Others are learning how to get along with other children, and still others are trying to understand what it means to be a participating member of a classroom community. This is the case throughout the elementary school years. Children develop skills when their brains and bodies are ready to develop those skills and not before.

When children can experience age-appropriate challenges during their growing-up years, they develop self-confidence and enjoy school and life. When they are expected to follow the rules before they've had a chance to learn and understand them, when they are expected to be quiet, stifle their natural curiosity, and act like little adults, they are miserable little people.

School is the work of children in this age group. They look up to their teachers, and they want to please them. Given encouragement and interesting material, they will enjoy learning. Children at this age benefit from lessons that involve movement, choice, and experimentation. They can be motivated by a smiley face drawn at the top of the page or a celebration of a perfect spelling test upon their arrival home.

FEEDBACK AND PRAISE

Somehow feedback and praise have been confused. The purpose of praise is to reward good work resulting in positive outcome and of course to encourage more good work. The purpose of good, clear feedback is not to make a child feel better when she gets something wrong. It is to help her do better when she makes a mistake or has put forth less than her best effort. When a child is told that her answer is wrong and she is asked to go back and think about it again, she might confuse this with some type of harsh judgment. She might believe that if she gives an answer—regardless of whether it's correct or not—she's done her part.

Her parent or teacher might want to protect her feelings and consequently try to soften the impact of feedback by combining it with empty praise. When adults do that, the child can choose to accept the praise and ignore the feedback. When a teacher says, "Great job! Do you think you can write in complete sentences?" a child will hear, "Great job," and dismiss the request to improve.

Instead, when an adult says, "Your handwriting is neater this time, but you need to write in complete sentences," the child is faced with a call to do better or more. This is specific, positive feedback, and it tells the child exactly what she did well and what she needs to do to produce good work.

Teachers and parents can get caught up in accepting and even praising minimal effort. Soon, all work is acceptable regardless of whether it involves hours of work and creativity or a quick search on Wikipedia. This approach eliminates the second half of the process of making mistakes. The child never gets a chance to ask, "If the answer is wrong, why is it wrong?" or "I haven't done this well, so what do I need to change? What do I need to do to make this really good?"

When your child has a written assignment and you see that his answer is garbled, asking him, "What is it that you're saying here?" will leave him with the burden of explaining himself more clearly. You haven't knocked all the wind out of his sails, and you haven't permanently damaged his fragile ego. You have simply asked him to express himself in a way that you can understand. It's good for children to be challenged to do better. That's the only way they can learn to do better.

THE SELF-ESTEEM MYTH

There has been a lot written about building children's self-esteem. Parents are told what to say to their children and how to say it so that they will foster self-esteem in their children. The thinking is that, if you focus on telling your precious little ones how handsome or beautiful they are, how talented they are, how smart and clever they are, then they will come to feel pretty good about themselves, and they will take risks, be successful, and of course be happy.

Current thinking goes something like this: If Tommy writes his name upside down and backward, mom should not correct him; rather she should marvel at his inventiveness. It doesn't matter that he is in third grade and should have learned to write his name correctly by now. It matters that he feels good about himself and his ability to write his name, despite all evidence to the contrary.

The trouble with this approach is that children are smarter than the theorists think they are. Tommy knows he is not writing his name correctly. Trophies for everyone don't convince the kids on the losing team that they won the game. Children know when they have worked hard to accomplish a task, and they know when they haven't. They also know when their good efforts have paid off and when they've lost despite giving their best. When your child feels guilty and frustrated because he didn't prepare for his test or didn't practice for that recital, you can help him to transform those emotions into motivation to do better next time.

You don't have to try to convince him that he did a great job. If you try, he will either think you've lost your mind or that you can't be trusted to help him figure out how to do better. You can encourage him to discard the guilt he feels for a half-hearted or ill-prepared effort by focusing on what can be done differently next time.

When your child has given it great effort and has still come up short, you can suffer with him as he acknowledges that his hard work wasn't enough to achieve the victory he sought. This is the moment when both of you have to acknowledge that, despite what popular culture may communicate, sometimes you cannot do whatever you set your mind to do. So you face that reality and let your child decide what to do next.

Children can learn how to evaluate their efforts and results, and they can make the connection between the two. With your help, they can assess their strengths and their weaknesses. With your encouragement, they will try again, and they will come to expect themselves to give only their best efforts as they work toward an important goal.

UNFOUNDED PRAISE

It's hard to allow your children to struggle and fail. At the same time, you know that you really only learn and feel that great sense of accomplishment after you have worked hard toward a goal. Everyone appreciates a genuine acknowledgment for a job well done. Self-esteem is not the goal—and it is certainly not given. No amount of empty praise can come close to matching the exhilaration that comes with a victory hard earned.

There are hazards inherent in providing unfounded praise in order to make your child feel better about herself. Telling your budding actress that she did a great job onstage despite the fact that she forgot her lines and spoke in a whisper is foolish, and she knows it. Instead, praising the fact that she swallowed her fear and stepped onto that stage makes more sense. If she wants to continue her acting career, she will need to discover what it takes to get better at the job. You can encourage her to do that without fake accolades.

When you tell your child that he is very special or that everything he does is awesome, you set him up for a hard fall. Reality will eventually slap him in the face, and he will be unprepared because you fooled him. Of course, you think your children are amazing and very special, but if you look, you can also see that they need to do more work to produce something really good, let alone something awesome.

If you can help your children to figure out how to create small victories—memorizing five lines at a time or catching five fly balls in a row—you will convince them that more is possible, and they will see that practice pays off. They will keep trying.

TRYING TO MAKE IT EASY

If you attempt to protect your children from every disappointing grade, every coach who expects them to practice harder, and every teacher who requires better behavior from them, they will miss the opportunity to examine the impact they have on others and the consequences of what they choose to do and not do. You will whisk away their chance to learn how to work with someone who doesn't already think they're perfect. You are a grown-up, after all. You're supposed to know how to tie your shoes, find the product in a multiplication problem, interview for a job at the local drugstore, and remember to bring your lunch when you go to work. When you do everything for your children, the only lesson they learn is that you know how to do things and they don't.

It is unfair to set your children up for mediocrity. If you never teach them the necessary connection between hard work and success, then they believe that success is beyond their control and is either owed to them or unattainable. Very early in their lives little children develop what is known as an internal locus of control—a sense that they can affect outcomes by what they do. If you've convinced them that they are owed a ticker-tape parade when they half-finish a task, then you may suddenly hear them whine, "It's not fair"— that they didn't get first place or an A or the prize they wanted. They don't understand that accomplishment and success actually require hard work.

As children move into the middle grades—third, fourth, and fifth—the academic, social, and extracurricular opportunities become more complex. In your child's classroom, there are children who have varying backgrounds and who have been exposed to far different levels of information. These children might have a store of information to share with classmates, but they may also have trouble listening when the teacher is teaching. There are children who have difficulty focusing or attending to the material at hand due to anxiety or worries about their home situation. These children are at a significant disadvantage when they try to focus on the instruction they are receiving.

If your family is experiencing any type of turmoil or upset, then it is important to remember that your child's participation in the educational process may well be hindered. Sometimes it helps to let teachers know if there is upset at home for whatever reason, and sometimes it will require that you provide additional academic support for your child at home.

INCREASING ACADEMIC EXPECTATIONS

During these middle-grade years, your child is bombarded with new information. She will begin the sometimes challenging task of prioritizing the information she receives and deciding what to attend to and what to discard. She will need to begin organizing her life around school, home, and the larger world. Homework expectations will increase, and she will have tests. Depending on classroom culture, tests can become very stressful for students.

FOCUSING ON OUTCOMES AND CHEATING

During these middle-grade years, children often become hyperfocused on outcomes. They are increasingly aware of how they are performing academically with respect to their classmates. This focus on outcomes can lead to pressure and fear. Your child might be fearful of disappointing you with a poor grade on a test. She might become anxious because she feels unprepared for an assessment. She might cheat on her test by looking at a classmate's paper. Your son might have forgotten about an assignment that is due today. He might worry that the teacher will call and tell you he is not handing in his work. He might ask a classmate to give him the answers to the assignment. Both children know that it's unlikely they will get caught cheating. They have seen other students cheat and get away with it numerous times. They have seen students get caught and not suffer any consequences.

If you become aware that your child has cheated or has even considered cheating, you need to make a big deal of it. This is one of those times when making a big deal of something relatively small will help you and your child avoid something much bigger in the future. He needs to know that whether he gets caught or not is not the point. The point is that he is not a boy who cheats. He needs to know that if he cheated to avoid doing poorly on a test, then you and he will engage in an examination of cause and effect. You will figure out if he knew he would fail due to poor preparation. That cause is easy to remedy. Asking, "What did you do or not do to prepare for this test?" and following up with "What will you do or not do differently next time?" can help your child take control of this problem. If her anxiety about failing the test got the better of her and caused her to believe she needed to cheat, then it might be a little harder to address, but it can be handled.

The outcomes of a cheating episode will need to be concrete, swift, and ongoing. Your child needs to know that cheating under any circumstances is unacceptable. She needs to know that honesty is not a relative concept and that her integrity is not dependent on the circumstances or what happens to other children who cheat. "Everybody does it" is not an acceptable excuse for any behavior. It is essential for your child to understand that poor preparation, disorganization, and anxiety do not excuse dishonesty. She also must recognize that these problems can be addressed.

Finally, you will need to explore how your child's desire to learn the material presented to them relates to her focus on outcomes and comparing herself with others. Is it possible that she is feeling overwhelmed and embarrassed because she is aware that she cannot keep up with her classmates? She may become fearful that others will discover her inability to retain or understand the material. This can lead her to experience increased stress and become so anxious that she is unable to demonstrate any learning.

LEARNING DISABILITIES

One of the most difficult things a parent can hear is that his child might have a learning disability or might need to be retained (school terminology for staying back a grade) because she hasn't been able to "meet the objectives of second grade." Even if you have been concerned about your son's struggles with reading, even if you have been spending several hours a night helping your daughter get through thirty minutes' worth of homework, once a school administrator or a teacher puts the struggle into words, it can be hard to swallow.

It is during these middle-grade years that students who have learning differences usually are identified and recommended for evaluation by outside service providers or the school district. Often in these conversations, teachers and administrators will hear for the first time that a mother has been spending hours trying to reteach material that her child missed, that she has been doing homework for her child because she didn't want her to fail, or that homework every night was a time of tears and frustration for her child.

This can be a difficult time for a child who struggles to keep up, as others begin to recognize and acknowledge what she has known for a while—that she can't do everything she's being asked to do. It can also be a relief for her to know that there is assistance available and that something will be done to help her.

Children who are encouraged to become familiar with their learning differences—and to see them as differences rather than as shortcomings or disabilities—can learn to recognize when they need help, how to get the help they need, and what works for them. As a parent, you might have to readjust your vision of success. If you can consider continued progress to be success, then you will be able to celebrate small victories and release your child from the obligation to be the best at something. This is the time to introduce the concept that there are many paths to the same goal. Use Waze and its alternate-route option as an example. It may take a little while longer to get to the destination if you take the scenic route, but you will see something new each time you go.

There are times when parents don't want to consider the possibility that their child has a learning problem. Maybe the parents are not interested in hearing about the testing or evaluation that can be done. At those times, parents have the final say. The teacher can still provide valuable help by creating reasonable limits on the amount of homework the child is required to do. She can set a time limit for all homework and alter some assignments so that the child doesn't get increasingly discouraged.

Eventually, the parents might come around and decide to pursue an evaluation, or the child might figure out how to keep up with the material. Until then, it is not the job of educators to penalize a child because her parents are not ready to explore the question of a learning difference. Teachers should provide whatever help they can to support her and her parents.

It can be difficult to accept that your child might face obstacles as she does her best to learn what she needs to learn. It can be hard for parents who found school easy and even fun to understand a child who dreads going to school because she finds herself unable to understand the lessons taught. If you struggled in school, you may see the pattern repeating itself and instantly remember how you felt as if you were always treading water, fearing that you could never catch up to your peers. If you acknowledge your frustrations and your sadness, then you can move on to become an advocate for your child, teaching her and others to see her learning differences as differences and not shortcomings or disabilities.

Matty

Matty was in fourth grade. His parents were divorced, and he lived with his dad half the week and his mom the other half. Every night, Matty was expected to get on IXL, a math review program, on the computer. The beauty of the program was that it let teachers know what lesson the student was on, how much time he spent on the review each night, and even what time of night he got on to work. Matty's teacher noticed that, when he was at his dad's house, Matty did not log on to the program. She also noticed that he did the whole week's work when he was at his mother's house, but he logged on at midnight or 1:00 a.m. when he did it.

The teacher called the parents for a conference. It turned out that Dad was completely unaware that Matty had this nightly assignment. When the teacher told Matty's mother that she was very concerned about Matty being up at midnight or 1:00 a.m. working on his IXL when he was with her, Mom insisted that that was impossible because Matty went to bed at 9:00 p.m. and she did not let him take the computer in his room. She was caught! Matty's mom had to admit that she was doing Matty's math homework at night. He found it too difficult or he was too tired to do it, so she did it for him "so he wouldn't get behind."

Matty needed to be evaluated, first by his teacher, then by a school administrator, to see if he was capable of learning the material as it was being presented or if he truly was unable to do the work his mother had been doing for him. As it turned out, with some cooperation between parents and an agreement that they would both work with Matty on his math, he was able to successfully complete his math objectives.

PARENTING A CHILD WITH A LEARNING DIFFERENCE

When you are the parent of a child with a learning or living difference (disability), you become more than a parent. You become an advocate for your child, and you become an expert. You research, and you learn everything you can about the diagnoses or labels that professionals have placed on your child, whether it be Down syndrome, attention deficit hyperactivity disorder, cerebral palsy, autism spectrum disorder, dyslexia, or any one of hundreds of other options. Once you've educated yourself, you look at your child with as much objectivity as you can muster, and you decide if the label fits.

Sometimes, it's undeniable, and you have no choice but to accept and move forward. If you're not sure or if you're positive the diagnosis is not correct for your child, then you will need to summon the courage to say so and seek a second or even third opinion.

If you and the experts agree that your child has a significant learning or living difference, you study the information available. Take, for example, a diagnosis of autism spectrum disorder. What exactly is it, and which signs, symptoms, possible complications, and characteristics of this diagnosis do you see in your child? Which can you say are not part of the picture of your child? There will be some of each. You prioritize. You decide what to tackle first. You ask yourself, "What is most getting in the way of my child enjoying a full and productive life today, and what do I anticipate will be an obstacle down the road?" You can make a good effort to anticipate what will make it most difficult for him to engage in a positive way with other people and the world around him. Sometimes you'll be right, and sometimes you won't. As with every important decision you make regarding your child, there are no guarantees.

Once you've decided on a primary issue, you will likely hit the books and the clinics, doctors, specialists, and therapists armed with your intimate knowledge of your child and your newfound knowledge of this disability that has been thrown into your life. You can ask a million questions about ways to adapt, services to access, and people to trust. This part can be really hard because every therapist, doctor, clinician, and educator you talk to will believe that what they have to offer should take priority. This is when you decide which direction to take first because you know your child better than anyone.

At some point—usually in the dead of the night—you probably will accept that he will not be like everyone else, that there is no cure for this, and hopefully you will decide that you will not twist and bend him to make him just like everyone else. You will need time to mourn the loss of a dream. Knowing you don't have much time, you will need to move on because there is work to do. You can set your mind and your heart on a path to do what it takes to help your child engage in a positive way with the world and the people in it. You know you want him to experience a sense of fulfillment in school and work that will make his life meaningful. You accept that his experiences will not be like most people's, but they will be his.

Joey

Joey was in preschool when the teachers first mentioned the word *evaluation*. They told Mom that Joey had some unusual behaviors that they thought might be indicative of a "problem." She knew what they were talking about. Joey was quirky. He didn't like it when people got too close to him, he rocked and hummed as he played by himself, and he rarely looked at her or engaged in conversation. He repeated particular phrases, and when it got a little noisy, he flapped his hands and then covered his ears.

After visits to the pediatrician, a developmental pediatrician, and a clinic, Joey was diagnosed with autism spectrum disorder. He began attending the clinic every afternoon. While there, he underwent examinations, evaluations, testing, and more. Joey tolerated the attention and the intrusions in his life pretty well; his mother, not so much. She was often angry and frustrated by what seemed like too many tests, too many questions, and too much emphasis on the things Joey couldn't or didn't do.

It was painful to see one specialist after another point out all the quirky, abnormal things that Joey did and all the "normal" things he apparently could not do. She felt like she had to put some normalcy back into Joey's life. She let the teachers at Joey's preschool know that he would be returning to school and would attend every day for a half-day. He would leave school after lunch for the clinic, where he would work with the specialists. The director of the preschool asked Joey's mom to come in for a conference before he returned.

Joey's mom silently received the information that they were "not equipped to serve Joey" and that they felt another placement would be "more appropriate." She left the director's office without a word, got in her car, and cried for thirty minutes. She wiped her tears and determined that she would never be taken by surprise again. She would find a school for Joey where he would be welcomed and learn with all kinds of children. She did just that. After lots of conversations and a good number of rejections, Joey's mom found a small parochial school where he was welcomed and supported.

Joey's mother continued to advocate for him until he reached adulthood. She was not always gentle and patient with Joey because she knew the world would not always be gentle and patient with him. She taught him to keep pushing himself even when it felt like the effort wasn't worth it. She worked with therapists and specialists, challenging them to capitalize on Joey's strengths and find ways around the things that got in his way.

Her mother's radar became refined and exact. She knew when someone was a true friend to Joey, and she knew when people were putting on an act. She helped Joey to connect with people who valued him, and she steered him away from the fakes. Sometimes people said she was too direct, too harsh, too demanding. Lots of people had ideas about how she should have raised Joey or how she could have institutionalized Joey and gotten on with her own life.

Joey's mom was too busy being Joey's mom to pay that much attention. When Joey got his first job and then his first apartment in a supportive living community, Joey and his mom popped a bottle of champagne and celebrated all that he had accomplished. As she left his apartment that night, Joey's mom said a little prayer of thanks for all that Joey had accomplished, full of hope for Joey's future.

Christian

Christian, a seven-year-old first-grader, was the youngest of four children His siblings were much older than he, in high school and college. In March of his first-grade year, the teachers expressed concern that Christian was not meeting most of the academic objectives for first grade. He was a sociable boy, a happy soul, kind and concerned about his classmates, but not at all interested in academics. He followed the rules, and he never misbehaved in class. He could sit in his seat, and he did not display any signs of attention disorders or other learning disabilities. He just hadn't progressed in the academic arena.

His teachers and the academic support team felt that another year in first grade would allow Christian the time he needed to meet the academic objectives. They met with his mom and shared their thoughts with her. She told them, "No, he should go forward to second grade. All of my kids were slow to develop. He'll be the same." Christian went on to second grade and beyond, and at the end of each year, his teachers expressed their concerns that he was behind in academics. Every year he squeaked by, and every year his mom assured everyone that he would be fine.

Christian never developed a negative attitude about school. He was kind and respectful, and he loved helping his teachers and the staff of the school. When he was at aftercare, he helped with the younger children, often leaving his homework for "later."

When Christian was ready to go to high school he was accepted to a local coed Catholic high school. He took his positive attitude and kind and accepting nature to school with him, and he instantly became a favorite of teachers and students. He grew into a fine young man, confident and articulate. He wasn't on the honor roll, but as he matured, he learned to work hard enough in school to pass his classes. He was on the soccer team, and he participated in extracurriculars throughout his four years.

Traditional teaching and learning involve three standard steps—teachers must deliver instruction, students and teachers must engage with the material, and students must be able to demonstrate learning. When Christian got to high school, it became evident that he had received the instruction and had engaged with the material—he had learned most of what he was taught. It just took a while before he was able to demonstrate his learning.

BOYS IN SCHOOL: SQUARE PEGS IN ROUND HOLES

The middle-grade years can be particularly difficult for boys. Being well-behaved students can take a lot out of many boys. Classrooms have rows of desks or pods, placing children in close proximity to one another—never good for wiggly boys. Sometimes, to keep misbehavior to a minimum, teachers sit the "naughtiest" boys next to the girls who are perfectly well behaved. This is particularly unfair to those little girls, who probably get knots in their stomachs worrying about what will happen if their charge doesn't have a pencil or can't manage to stay in his seat.

School can become a place where many boys find that they cannot do any-thing right—meaning they cannot act like girls and follow the female rules established by female educators. Their constant missteps can lead to shame and frustration and eventually to a complete disconnect from the teacher and even school itself. Because everything they do tends to be larger and louder and more direct than it would be if done by girls, many boys can be faced with harsh and frequent discipline. It's your job to teach your sons how their behavior might affect others. You don't want to go so far as to "un-boy" them, but you do want to help them discern when, with whom, and where their humor and activity are acceptable.

Boys are at least twice as likely to be diagnosed with attention disorders, learning disabilities, autism, and emotional disabilities. They are more likely to be victims of physical abuse and violence than girls. Boys hear less. They are often affected by background noise distracting them from hearing what they need to hear. They receive visual information better when it is presented on their left side. When faced with a task, boys' brains turn on for those tasks and then turn off—this differs from girls who generally remain "on" for most of the school day. This means that, after boys have finished that math work-sheet, many find something interesting to do over in the corner. Then they're startled to hear that classwork has continued without them. Children cannot learn from teachers they don't trust, teachers who don't get them, or teachers who don't like them. Boys need to know three things in the classroom: the objective, the rules, and who's in charge. Once they know, with some coach-ing, they can adapt, behave, and engage in the learning process.

Most boys need physicality. They need regular movement breaks when they are in school all day, and they need to play outside. Their energy is con-tagious (to other boys). They are sometimes oblivious to risk. They usually are direct (oftentimes seen as rude). They often have a strong sense of justice and fairness. They can be gross, tender, and totally unpredictable. Boys tend to love competition and horseplay. They typically are concrete thinkers who don't hold grudges, and they usually are intensely loyal. These qualities can be transformed into liabilities by educators who fail to understand them.

Sitting still and facing front, raising hands but not too high, reading aloud but not calling out, listening to whole-class instruction, and working quietly at one's desk—none of these work well for most boys. Consequently, many of them click pens, chew pencil erasers, shave their pencils down with the edge of their rulers, doodle, stare at posters on the wall, look out the window, get up to sharpen pencils, get a tissue, throw out trash, or go to the bathroom instead of learning what is being taught.

Don't be fooled, though; they are learning. The trouble is that they might be learning that their natural instincts are not acceptable in a classroom set-ting. They could be learning to avoid or barely tolerate instruction until the bell rings to set them free—at least for a while. Is it any wonder that children are throwing Cheetos at one another during lunch or eating so fast that they cannot digest their lunch before charging out the doors to the playground? Is it any wonder that they are so intense on the basketball court or when playing touch football that they end up wrestling with an opposing player and then getting sent to the principal's office? There they end up sitting out the remainder of their free time before reluctantly heading back into a classroom where they are expected to sit for another couple of hours.

There are certainly girls who would prefer to move around the classroom and girls who are not comfortable sitting through lessons with no break. Those girls need movement breaks and recess as much as any of the boys. There are also girls who find themselves distracted by the view out the window or an especially good book that they have hidden in their laps. They may not be as disruptive in the classroom, but they are equally tuned out. Teachers who recognize that students in this age group need lessons that include movement, physical engagement, lively discussion, and lots of variety will serve all their students well.

RECESS

Recess is important to all children, whether they are playing a wild game of soccer or basketball, sitting in a circle talking, looking for bugs or pretty leaves, or just wandering around quietly. So much learning happens during recess!

Children begin to discover how they fit into the larger society of children in their school. Are they welcomed to join a group, or are they excluded for some reason? Are they leaders or followers? Can they get along with others, even when things get competitive or when they don't get their way? These questions are answered on the playground and in the cafeteria more than anywhere else.

When teachers keep boys or girls inside during recess because of behaviors or because work is not completed, they fail to realize how important it is for children to have time to compete in a playground game, to run off excess energy, or to talk to their friends. This tortuous restriction only serves to foster resentment among children who are already having trouble meeting the restrictive requirements of the average fourth- or fifth-grade classroom.

The same teacher who uses recess as punishment will wonder at the end of the day why the wonderful lessons he had planned for the afternoon failed so miserably. He never realizes that they failed because he was trying to teach students who needed time to be active and needed to take a break and not sit still for hours without fresh air or exercise. As it turns out, he punished himself and the rest of the class by punishing those students.

Timmy and Eddie

Timmy and Eddie were third-grade friends. They loved playing soccer during recess every day. Both boys were very competitive and pretty hot-tempered. As often happened when they were on opposing teams, Timmy and Eddie got into a scuffle when they disagreed about a play. The young teacher on recess duty was appalled to see them rolling around in the dirt, and she almost fainted when Eddie came out of the scrum with a bloody nose. She sent Eddie and Timmy to the nurse and told them to report to the principal afterward. Meanwhile, she used her walkie-talkie to tell the principal she was sending two boys up for "fighting" on the playground. After getting cleaned up by the nurse, the boys reluctantly sat on the bench outside the principal's office, hoping that she might not notice they were there.

By the time she opened her door, both boys were close to tears, fearing that they would be banned from recess for the rest of their lives. When they were asked to recount the "fighting" incident, neither boy could remember exactly what happened before they were apprehended by the teacher.

"Was it a pretty intense game?" the principal asked. They assured her that it was.

"Was it fun?" she asked. They assured her that it was.

"Are you two still friends?" she asked. They assured her that they were.

"Do you think Timmy made your nose bleed on purpose?" she asked Eddie. Looking incredulous, Eddie told her that he thought it started bleeding when he hit it on the ground and that was not Timmy's fault.

"Shake hands," said the principal. So they did, both grinning a little.

"Have some M&Ms and try not to upset the teachers by fighting anymore," she said. They each took a handful of M&Ms and looked at her expectantly.

"Well," she said, "hurry up. You have five minutes of recess left."

QUIET BOYS AND GIRLS

What of the boys who are quiet or small in stature or who have no interest in athletics? These boys might feel far safer in the classroom than in the lunchroom or on the playground. They might take a book outside with them or befriend a group of girls who prefer swings and chatter to competition on the fields.

They are at risk of being teased and even bullied if the adults around them don't ensure that they can safely engage with friends and in activities with which they are comfortable. Insisting that the boys play with the boys puts these guys in a tough spot, and it's just one more way to make their lives difficult. One day they may decide that they will play with the boys, but until they are ready, there is no need to force them into situations that are uncomfortable for them.

The quiet girls who haven't yet developed strong communication skills or who are just not able to keep up with the fast-paced chatter in and out of the classroom can feel isolated and invisible. These girls might spend most of their day hoping to go unnoticed. They should be allowed to be quiet. Not everyone needs to be a go-getter or a leader. Calling on these girls when they are unprepared is not fair. Teachers can, though, encourage their participation by warning quiet students ahead of time that she will ask them a specific question.

There is, of course, other learning that takes place in school—at least we hope there is! When it comes to writing essays or stories, children's brains are almost overflowing. They have so many great ideas that can get completely jammed up and never make it to the paper. The inability to parse their ideas out slowly can keep young students from even beginning a writing assignment. Allowing students to dictate their ideas into a program that types their words will give them a good start on telling their stories. They should be expected to go back and edit their work, but this is much more acceptable once they've gotten their ideas out of their heads.

Asking children to read quietly in a classroom where every sound indicates that there is something interesting happening elsewhere puts them in a tough spot. As an alternative, a teacher can read to the class as the students follow along, and boys and girls alike can enjoy what is being read and can glean far more information from a read chapter than they can from one they read themselves.

This is not to say that young students can't read or shouldn't be encouraged to read. Rather, they will get much more from their reading when they do it in a quiet room where they are comfortable. Oral reading or round-robin reading are done largely for the teacher's benefit. It is a form of assessment of reading skills, but it is a faulty one. Children who read fluently and comprehend well can also be anxious oral readers and appear to be unable to manage the text.

What about math? Many boys are more comfortable with the concrete, measurable, definitive material of math and science, and many girls need additional support when it comes to math. Almost all children will enjoy measuring, weighing, timing, and manipulating at home. Ask your child to measure the area of the family room, and then determine what size rug you should order. Buy him a stopwatch, and you will find that he is timing everything he does and maybe everything you do. Ask him to set a timer for the cake that's in the oven. Don't let Alexa do it! Then ask him what time it will be when the cake is done. Pick up an abacus at a local yard sale and see what kind of fun he can have using it for his math facts review.

GIRLS IN SCHOOL: THE SWEET SPOT

Most girls in these middle grades are comfortably in their zone. They value neatness and academic achievement. They raise their hands to answer questions, and they are rewarded with responsibilities in the classroom. They organize the papers, and they pass the papers—both jobs that provide them an opportunity to move around. (Boys should be given these jobs, too!)

Girls in the middle grades can and should thrive in the classroom and in their extracurricular activities. This is a time of tremendous learning for them. Their experiences in school, on teams, in activities, and in the larger community should be exciting and fun. Parents need to tune in and encourage their children to pursue activities that interest them. If your daughter can play on an athletic team or participate in the band or choir, she can build her confidence level as she works with others to achieve a goal. Her sense of control over her life will increase, and she will very likely have fun.

Involving girls in the middle grades in projects that make use of their natural talents and their need to belong to a group—collecting food items for a pantry, helping younger students in the school library or on holiday projects, collecting items for soup kitchens or maternity homes—all of these can highlight girls' talents and strengths and reinforce their sense of belonging, making it less likely that they will engage in relational bullying.

While boys can feel that they are being penalized by teachers and school administrators simply because they are boys who are full of energy and still believe firmly that their developing physical acumen is leading them right to the NBA or the NFL, girls may be thriving in the classroom but struggling on the playground or in the cafeteria. They may face some resistance from adults and even some ridicule from peers if they pursue athletics with intensity, if they decide to withdraw from physical activity, or if they try to speak up or speak out against a perceived injustice.

Girls who prefer to sit quietly and read or who have limited access to social media may be completely overlooked by the children and adults in their lives. They can begin to feel invisible and completely unknown. Making sure that your child has an opportunity to spend time with one or two friends is important if she's quiet or if she is not as sophisticated as many of her classmates. It will also be very important to provide quiet children with an opportunity to talk about their experiences at home. Patiently waiting and listening without rushing or interrupting will help them to become comfortable sharing their stories.

CHOOSING THE RIGHT SCHOOL

Children are meant to love school. They have a natural curiosity about the world, people, the past, and the future. They want opportunities to talk about things, and they thrive on new information. You will need to be vigilant about choosing the right school environment for your child. You are his best advocate because you know him better than anyone. When you advocate for him, you will need to be direct and straightforward with teachers and coaches, but you also need to be realistic. You can't, and you shouldn't, defend every misbehavior or make excuses for every missed assignment. You certainly won't assume that the teacher dislikes your child because she doesn't tolerate his sometimes rambunctious behavior in the classroom. You will, though, discover the ways in which the teacher and the school support boys and make learning possible for them.

It is your responsibility to stay tuned in to your child's school and social experiences, making sure that you provide multiple opportunities for him to talk about his struggles, victories, and the things he is learning about the world and himself. He won't necessarily want you to provide answers to his dilemmas for him, nor will he want you to step in and solve his problems, but he will probably let you if you decide to take over his life. So hold strong. Listen. Ask questions.

Ask, "What do you think you could say to your teacher about that?" or "How are you planning to handle that?" Maybe you can relate (briefly!) an instance when you faced a similar situation. Then, if she asks, you can tell her what you did and whether it worked well or not. Most of the time, it works better if you tell her about a time when you took action and it didn't come out the way you wanted. Then you don't sound like the expert; you sound more like somebody who understands the struggle.

In a lot of ways, these years between five and ten are years of delightful innocence, when children still like sharing stories about their days and they are learning hundreds of things about themselves and their world every day. They laugh and cry readily. They seem to grow inches in days, or they look like they will never grow at all. They want to please you. They want you to think they are the greatest kid ever. They want to be near you, and they want you to protect them from growing up too fast.

Chapter 8

Family Life of Tweens, Ages Ten to Fourteen

So you've got a good system going at home. Your children understand that they are contributors to the well-being of the family. They are happy in school, and they love to tell you long, rambling stories about their days. They sometimes do the dishes and most often pick up their messes, and you continue to support their efforts to do a great job. They usually listen when you talk, and they almost never talk back. Your child is maturing nicely. You are doing a heck of a job!

Then they get to middle school. The middle school years are awkward and exciting, filled with fun and angst for children and parents. School days are filled with hundreds of tiny social exchanges—looks between boys and girls, smiles, laughter, awkward conversations, burning red ears, tears that appear without warning, secrets shared, and lessons learned and unlearned at a rapid-fire pace.

SOCIAL SKILLS

Your child might be trying out new personalities, often on a weekly basis. One week, your daughter may decide she wants four or five new piercings and wants to wear all black. She might talk about dying her hair, using the words *purple* and *orange*. The very next week, she could let you know she wants to stop into J.Crew to check out those cute madras shorts, and her long braids remain intact. You can learn to ride out the change waves, nodding your head and saying, "Hmm," a lot.

Because a few of the girls told him he looks like Brad Pitt, your son may become quite certain that he's headed for the big screen and ask about acting lessons and head shots one week. Soon after, he can be focused solely on dribbling with his left hand in anticipation of college basketball scouts arriving any day, or he might let you know he is seriously considering just skipping college and going right to the NBA.

You can love his optimism and enthusiasm, and you can encourage his interest in so many diverse pursuits, but you'd best hold off on paying for an acting coach or a private trainer for the time being. You can also avoid the temptation to bring him back down to earth by telling him that, if he doesn't do his homework, he'll never even get into college, and if he doesn't shower soon, no one will remember that he looked like Brad Pitt because he smells so bad.

Right before your eyes they are growing up! While they certainly aren't there yet, progress is being made. You should feel pretty good about how this adolescent thing is going. You are learning to hand over some of the small responsibilities, and your child is happily stepping up to assume more responsibility for himself.

Reality intrudes. Suddenly, Mr. Maturity might leave his binder and all his homework in the car in the morning. Suddenly you might receive an email from the teacher that says your perfectly behaved daughter is "very chatty" during class. He wants his door shut. She wants a phone, and she wants to pick out her own clothes without your help. He either avoids bathing altogether or takes a shower twice a day without being told to. He hates girls today, and tomorrow he's besotted by the high school girl next door. These changes in mood, interests, and circumstances can make you and your child feel like you're on a roller coaster. Try to hold on tight!

When he stumbles in the door after school, weighed down by his enormous backpack, and he heads for the kitchen and eats like he has not eaten in weeks, you might be tempted to ask questions about his day. Between Oreos and oranges, he will likely grunt and mumble one-word answers. You will get very little information, and what you do get will be hard to understand. Soon he'll be on his way to his room, where he will close the door and hide out until suppertime. Try not to get your feelings hurt. Your children need time after school to process all that they have encountered during the day. It's tough work navigating the world of a middle schooler.

When she does feel ready to talk, be sure you listen, even when it seems that she is talking about something small and insignificant. The small things are the important things. She puts them out there to better understand the bigger things that surround her. Listen and affirm. No need to offer suggestions unless you are specifically asked. Try not to criticize your daughter or anyone else in the scenario being described. Your judgment could be just enough to make her reluctant to tell you her story next time. Consider each of these conversations the gift that it is.

If your daughter talks about a friend she is fighting with, you might find yourself wondering how to soothe the tears of the sobbing child in front of you. Chances are, if you agree that Susie is just mean and confide that you never thought she was such a good friend, your daughter will look at you like you've gone insane. Suddenly she is defending her friend! What she's really doing is defending herself and her choice of Susie as a best friend. Your daughter tells you her story in a simple attempt to connect with you and to understand better what's happened between her and her friend. Better to allow her to do the criticizing and chime in only when you have something positive to say.

LOSING TOUCH

Once they enter adolescence, tweens and their parents may express their closeness in new ways. But mothers and fathers can still communicate unconditional love for them. You may not hold them on your lap or snuggle with them on the couch, but you can get at least a couple of hugs a day and a kiss good night. You can demonstrate your affection for your son by straightening his collar or smoothing his hair, placing your hand firmly on his back as he goes off to school. They still need that human contact, just not in the same ways. Those few seconds when you look into his eyes and see the baby he was and the man he is becoming are shiny treasures to keep.

Middle school children may act like all human contact makes them uncomfortable, but that doesn't mean they don't want you to touch them. They want you to respect their self-consciousness, development, and privacy, but you are still their parent, so you get to give them a hug and a kiss on the cheek. Your pride in them, your interest in how their day has gone, and your willingness to listen to them communicate your love for them.

RAPID-FIRE CHANGES

Most girls are maturing into beautiful young ladies, and many boys are thickening up. Boys' shoulders are getting broader, they are developing muscles, they are getting taller, and of course, they are in the heat of puberty. Some boys get the shadow of a mustache, and most have heard more than once that they smell after PE class. They need to shower every day, sometimes twice a day. It's your job to tell them that and to get them some deodorant.

Some boys are the same height they were in third grade, and they are seeing no signs of puberty on the horizon. These boys can be victims of ridicule, or they can be completely ignored by their peers. Being ignored is probably preferable to most of them, as they can pretend that no one notices when they are behind in development. No matter who the boy is or where he is in puberty, your boy needs some strong relationships. He needs at least one in-person friend he can eat lunch with or walk to school with.

BOYS AND MEN

It is important for adolescent boys to have a strong bond with the important men in their lives, to see them as people to be admired and respected. They want to be able to look at their dad or their grandfather and recognize his goodness, integrity, and love for family. They need to be able to ask good men for advice, and they need to spend time having fun with their dads, grand-dads, uncles, and brothers. Boys who have an opportunity to learn about how their fathers and grandfathers grew up will come to appreciate the dramatic changes that have taken place in the world and in their dads' and granddads' lives. They can see that some things remain constants, however. They can learn to look out for friends and family. They will come to appreciate time spent talking about what came before as a way of understanding what is happening in the world today.

BOYS AND WOMEN

From the women in their lives, boys can learn to consider alternative perspectives on situations. As they witness conversations and discussions between their parents, they can begin to see that two people with different points of view or different priorities can still reach an agreement. They can learn that the respect of others is earned, and they can learn what it means to demonstrate respect for others. Boys can learn that gentleness and kindness are qualities that all people should develop.

MISSIONS FOR BOYS

Michael Gurian stresses that mission is an ongoing challenge.[1] In a world that emphasizes personal satisfaction, where so much focus is on the hunt for happiness, you will want to commit to making sure your kids know that they are not owed anything but the love of family and opportunities to do good work. Boys *want* to sacrifice for a cause. They want to hunt down the monsters. They want to be the hero who stands up for the little guy. They just need someone to expect it of them, and they will make their best attempt to be men of honor.

Douglas MacArthur wrote *Duty, Honor, Country* to the young men of the United States Military Academy.[2] These words embody the concepts of character and integrity that are so important to those who raise young men. If every parent of every boy took the time to read and talk about this speech with their sons—more than once—then their sons would understand what it means to be a man of integrity who serves others, develops his own God-given talents, and makes the world a better place.

Through your words and your actions, you can help your son to develop a sense of appreciation for his gifts and talents and to accept the responsibility he has to develop and use those gifts and talents. When he is inclined to feel sorry for himself for whatever reason, it's important to shut that down quickly. It is too easy in today's world to become a professional victim—of circumstance, of others' good luck, of unfair treatment, or of lack of talent.

BOYS AND THEIR EMOTIONS

While adolescent girls usually take the rap for being moody, boys at this age can be moody, too. They are more aware of academic expectations and struggles, they are more tuned in to family conflicts or financial struggles, and they are under pressure to be accepted by their peers. They worry about being made fun of for their size, their pimples, their clothes, even their shoes. They worry about getting in trouble at school, and they worry about what's coming when they get to high school.

These stressors can cause them to be on edge and testy over the simplest things. One minute your son can be laughing and joking in the kitchen while jamming string cheese in his mouth, and the next he can be sullen and silent, insisting on being alone. One of the saddest things to see is a boy who feels that it is unacceptable for him to cry. An adolescent boy may very well have the impression that, to be manly, he must restrain any emotions. The idea that being tough means denying feelings of sadness or fear comes to him from popular culture and sometimes from within his own family.

He can stuff his feelings down, refusing to acknowledge them, but those feelings will resurface somehow. They may show up in angry outbursts at school or at home. They may show up in mean comments, bullying of other children, self-harm, or excessive risk-taking behavior. Boys need to know from the important men and women in their lives that sadness and fear are part of life. Feelings are not meant to be the driving force behind everything they do, but they are not to be ignored. They are meant to be expressed, considered, and then kept in perspective.

Boys need to know that the world will not end if they cry. They can learn this from their dads and grandfathers. They can attend a funeral with their dad or have a heartfelt conversation about times when their dad was terribly sad. They need to know that good, strong men are afraid of things. They need to know that courage doesn't mean they aren't afraid; rather it means they will do the right thing despite being afraid.

Boys need to be recognized for their character and compassion. They need opportunities to make good decisions, and they need to be acknowledged when they've done that. It can be incredibly exciting and fulfilling to parent a boy as he enters adolescence and begins the process of becoming a good man.

COACHING GIRLS

Girls at this age seek meaning and purpose but in different ways. Your daughter needs opportunities to work with a team, to compete and collaborate, to accomplish something difficult. Don't overlook your girl's need to take risks, to do something outstanding. Traditionally (and sadly), for many years, the emphasis in raising girls has been on raising a good girl, a nice girl, a popular girl, or a polite girl. Of course you want her to be nice and polite but not at the expense of speaking her mind or pursuing a goal and championing a cause.

This is where it gets tough for lots of reasons. Mothers can over-identify with their daughters during the middle school years. It can be hard for some moms to accept that their daughters need to live their middle school years with their parents on the sidelines cheering them on and coaching them, not in front of them running interference. It can be just as difficult for dads to accept that their daughters are becoming young women who have opinions that they want to express.

Think of yourselves as soccer coaches. Your girl needs to know the rules. She needs to know her role on the team. She needs to know that you think she can do her job and do it well. She needs to know that you will coach her and pat her on the back when she messes up. She needs to know that you want her in the game. She needs to know that you will pull her out if she's not playing as well as you expect her to and you'll give her a chance to collect herself before she returns to the game.

Girls can learn so much from their mothers during the middle school years, and not all of it is about makeup and clothes. It is important for girls to understand the physiology and the implications of the physical and emotional changes they are experiencing. Parents should share stories of their own years in middle school—years without social media or cell phones, when you could walk anywhere you wanted to safely, when you felt self-conscious or awkward, when you first fell in love. These stories can connect you to your daughters in a very special way.

But girls can and should learn from their dads and brothers during this time. Shooting baskets, going fishing, and taking hikes or camping trips with the men in the family allow your daughter to abandon the need to be "girly." She can just be herself and face physical challenges, sweating and struggling with her male family members without embarrassment or cares. If Mom gets included in the next basketball game or takes part in the annual camping trip, then girls can see firsthand that everyone can enjoy making a layup or sitting around a campfire. Fathers, always cognizant of their daughters' need for privacy and respect, can still have fun with them and at the same time demonstrate the treatment girls should expect from boys and men.

HELP FROM ADULTS

As girls realize that their words can be used to hurt, they can also learn that their words will lift up and include others and that they are capable of creating solutions to difficult problems. With help from the adults in their lives, girls can begin to see themselves as a positive force, and they can begin to understand the potential this holds for their lives. They can read about and talk about women who have made a difference in the world, despite the odds. Give your girl the opportunity to admire the women in our history and in the world today who choose to travel their own paths, who are often laughed at or dismissed but have kept at it anyway. Go to movies, plays, and exhibits that feature stories of strong women. Together, read books about creative women.

None of the emphasis on strong women has to become a "put men down" campaign or a victim statement. It is not that at all. It is simply a way to show your daughter her potential, the possibilities, and the opportunities she has. Your girl can learn that she can shield herself and her friends from derision and minimization by uniting and by being successful—not by whining or claiming to be victims. Men are not the bad guys here. The real enemy is the girl's misperception that she lacks the power and the ability to speak out, to solve problems, to make changes, and to accomplish something amazing. When a girl sees herself as less than, when she feels that she cannot have an effect on her world, it might be because other girls have helped to convince her of that. Mean girls use their power to put down other girls. Those mean girls need to be told again and again that they are better than the behavior that they exhibit—that they have so much more to contribute than gossip, cruelty, or good looks.

Fathers, grandfathers, and brothers can have a significant impact on the way a girl grows up. It's not enough for them to say, "You can be anything you want to be," if they don't support and encourage her efforts to be assertive and to share ideas. Girls depend on encouragement from the men in their lives. They need to be encouraged to say what they think and to defend their positions in disagreements and discussions with males and females. Oftentimes, girls can find themselves screaming and crying or shutting down completely because they feel picked on or dismissed by louder, deeper, more resonant voices. The men in the house need to learn to control their voices, to wait, and to listen so that their girls can be heard.

Parents, show and tell your daughters exactly what you believe it means to be a strong and loving woman—a lot. Tell your girls that you want them to be compassionate and that compassion is not just a virtue—it requires action. You want them to know that judging one another by what they see on the outside is a terrible injustice. Girls can learn that no one knows what's behind the outfits or the behaviors and that it's not their job to judge other girls. They can come to realize that their power does not come from putting other girls down.

BEING HEROES

The reality is that young people yearn for meaning. They are waiting for their opportunity to be better. They want someone to expect them to be heroes. They want someone to teach them how to appreciate and sacrifice for a cause. You can take the following actions to help your child obtain that meaning:

- Point out a need. Point out the boy or girl who's being left out. Talk about how that person could be included without a big show.
- Say no. Tell your son to work for the money to buy that new lacrosse stick or basketball.
- Expect her to be grateful, strong, and kind. Don't accept less.
- Reset the management structure of the house. Be in charge. Release him from the need to be in charge of your family by refusing to give in to his demands.
- Remind her that you are her parent and you know her pure heart and soul. You know what she can be.
- Tell him you won't allow him to be less.
- Let her know that you are willing to go to any lengths to help her become the woman she is meant to be.
- Remind him every day to be grateful, to respect the people around him, and to see himself as a good person.

Boys and girls need to see what kindness and compassion look like in everyday life. If you try to do the ordinary things better, with gratitude for even the craziest days and an appreciation for the kindness of others, then you send a strong message to your children. If you work on becoming a better parent, friend, and spouse, then he will follow your example. Working together to be better, you can change the world. You can bring back the grace the world has lost. Give him the dream, and then work with him to make it true.

As you create a picture of humanity that allows for imperfections, you give your child a reason to be kind and to avoid judging other people. She will come to believe in the essential connectedness of all of humanity, including those who look and think like she does and those who do not. When you show your child that you do not place greater value on strong bodies and minds and that you do not pity those who look and speak differently, she will become more able to stand shoulder to shoulder with others. She can begin to see a bit of herself in other people and to see that differences make people interesting. When judgment is suspended, kindness will grow. In today's world, we can use all the kindness we can get.

GIVING CHILDREN WHAT YOU THINK THEY WANT

Many parents spend hours and hours working to earn enough to give their children everything. They are determined that their children will not be unhappy, and somehow, they come to believe that things will make their kids happy. The truth is that material possessions can never be an adequate substitute for time spent together doing nothing special. As a result of parental overindulgence, too many young people develop a sense of entitlement that can permeate every relationship they have. They think they deserve to have what they want when they want it. They don't know how to handle "no," and they have no interest in learning how to manage without the things they think they want.

This can be seen in classrooms, where teachers are treated as hired help. These are the children who demand that they receive the grade they want rather than the grade they earn. These children are rude in the classroom, engaging in conversations and other activities while teachers are trying to teach. They are the children who consider their own parents to be adjuncts who exist to meet their every need. These children don't just appear out of nowhere. Somewhere along the line, someone has not paid enough attention to the details. Someone has misunderstood the point of this parenting thing. Somewhere along the line, these children have gotten the message that they are, indeed, only as good as the things they have and the power they hold.

TEACHING BY EXAMPLE

Can you expect your children to know what a healthy relationship looks like? You can because you teach them what a real, respectful, loving relationship looks like. You are fighting against an avalanche of negative messages, but you cannot give up. Adolescents have radar, and they can tell a fake a mile away. They are watching every move the adults around them make, and they are listening to every word you say—to them and to other adults. If you don't live what you preach, then your children will learn that adults can be duplicitous, can favor some students over others, and can gossip and make fun of other people and still be well regarded.

When parents have respectful discussions and disagreements, children will learn that not every disagreement has to end with someone losing. They will see that two people who love and respect one another can disagree, compromise, and work things out. The relationship between a child's parents provides her with a model of what a respectful, adult relationship can be. If her parents operate as a team, share tasks, laugh together, express affection for one another, and treat one another with kindness and respect, then she will seek that in her relationships.

CIVILITY

Consistently teach your children to stand up tall, to look people in the eye, to shake hands, and to stand up when an adult walks into the room. If you speak to your children in complete sentences and expect complete sentences back from them, then this will be second nature to them. They will learn how to have a real conversation—not through text messaging or email. Teach them to sacrifice personal success for the good of the group.

Your tween should use titles: Mr., Mrs., or Doctor. She should say, "Yes, sir," and "Yes, ma'am," when addressing adults. She should hold the door and should step back and let others enter first. Your child should not raise her voice to her parents or any other adult. When she understands what it feels like to be a civilized and honorable person, it will be remarkably easy for her to be comfortable in any social situation.

What is the point of stressing old-fashioned civility? These behaviors speak loudly and clearly to other people and to your children themselves. They say, "This is who I am. This is from where and whom I come. I am confident. This is what I believe about myself and other people that we all deserve to be treated with respect."

Soon he will be the boy who volunteers to help, and he will do more than is expected. Your child will be grateful for what he has and for the people in his life who help him to grow up. He will be confident enough to be a friend and include others who might otherwise be left out. In order for this change to be effective, though, you will need to be as straight as the desert. You cannot waver. You cannot give in. Your child deserves that much from you. Don't give up on him because it's hard. Make a promise to your child and to yourself that you will do this right for him, and then keep your promise.

FAMILY MEALS

One of the best things you can do for your family is to schedule at least one meal together every day. It doesn't have to be dinner, if practices and homework get in the way. Maybe it's breakfast, which allows you to make sure everyone has a positive start to their day. Whichever meal it is, everyone should know ahead of time when you will come together to eat. Don't let devices, sullen teenagers, busy schedules, or other externals interfere with your designated time together.

Watch yourself during these meals, though. Avoid quizzing your children about their days or about their plans for the days and weeks ahead. Abandon the role of food police. He knows you want him to eat healthy, and one day he will. Have healthy food available, and sooner or later he will try it, or he won't.

Before you eat, express some gratitude for your family, the food, your life. Ask everyone at the table to join you and to offer some words of gratitude. Establish a tradition of doing this before meals, and your children will treasure that tradition. It is worth it—just wait and see.

Family, consistency, dependability, everyone contributing, able to count on one another—that's the key, isn't it? Family members need to not let one another down. Children want to know that their parents will be parents to them—always. You might not make every game or every concert. You might not be there every day when they get home from school because you have to work or travel. You might even raise your voice or lose patience or serve hot dogs with no vegetables. As long as your children know that you will love them no matter what, as long as they know you can be counted on, they will be fine.

Chapter 9

Social Life of Tweens, Ages Ten to Fourteen

WHERE DO I FIT IN?

This question is asked and answered in many ways for middle school children. Middle school children spend more time with their peers than they do with their parents. They are at school for eight hours, they might have two hours of practice or after-school clubs, and they attend lots of social events, most of which do not welcome adults.

Athletic and taller boys may move to the top of the pyramid, while small, quiet boys can become almost invisible in middle school. Girls can command attention and establish themselves as leaders—in positive or negative ways. If a girl's power rests in her ability to put other girls down, then she will be feared. If her power rests in her ability to include everyone and get along with everyone, then her power rests in her integrity, and the admiration of her classmates is sustained and well earned.

Because many middle school students no longer have recess at school—even though they still need a break from sitting in class and they still need to move—the hallways and the locker rooms replace the playground as socialization areas. It is in these spaces and the cafeteria that young people establish social connections and decide how they will relate to other kids. They also begin to see how other kids react to them, perhaps by attempting to join a group or begin a conversation. These areas are rarely monitored and can serve as breeding grounds for bullying and exclusion unless adults are present and vigilant.

You can help your children to navigate these sometimes treacherous waters by encouraging them to take their time, to watch, and to listen. Encourage them to look for the good guys—the guys who smile or make room for others to join them. Then, when your child has approached a group and been welcomed, she may want to bide her time—observing and listening—to see if these are the kinds of people she wants to be friends with. So often middle school students and their parents are anxious for them to belong to a group. But this process, if done well, takes time and thought. Give your child permission to be thoughtful about the new friends he makes.

DANCES AND DATING

Be sure that you volunteer to chaperone at the first dance so that you can see the setup and decide whether it's appropriate for your child. Remember, there is more than enough time for pitch-dark rooms and suggestive dancing when your child gets to high school. Try not to rush things because you think it's cute.

Children in middle school often decide that they should be "dating" someone. Essentially, dating in middle school means letting everyone know that two children have developed a fondness for one another. There are rarely actual dates. Trips to the movies with a group of friends or birthday and holiday parties provide tweens the opportunity to socialize in a relatively public setting. It will be important to monitor your tween's behavior during these years, as he may feel some pressure to engage in activities that are better suited for older teens or young adults.

The beauty of being a tween is the fact that tweens usually travel in packs. They feel more comfortable going to the mall eatery or the movies with a group of friends rather than with a boyfriend or girlfriend. Not all middle school students prefer to socialize in a larger group, however, and as long as a child is not feeling left out or excluded, this is fine. Many children prefer to travel light.

If your child has one or two good friends who seem like really nice kids, then encourage them to come to your house, take them to the movies or birthday parties, or arrange outings to the museums or just trips to the tennis courts or the park. As long as your child has one or two good in-person friends, she's not traveling alone.

BULLYING

It's a parent's nightmare, isn't it—that your child might be bullied at school? Who are the victims of bullying? It's hard to predict who will be chosen; sometimes kids are chosen for the most insignificant reasons: because they sit next to someone in class, because the teacher seems to favor them or doesn't seem to like them, because their parents are odd, because they get good grades, or because they get bad grades. It might be kids who struggle with social cues who can be bullied, kids who react strongly when teased, either getting angry or crying; children who dress differently; or kids who are seen as uncoordinated, overweight, underweight, shy, or annoying. They are all potential victims. Boys who are identified as unacceptable or uncool by the girls can become the victims of bullying by those girls and, soon, by the boys in the class who fear being labeled in the same way. What begins as relational bullying—the specialty of girls—can develop into physical torment and ostracism on the male side of the world.

The culture of exclusion and hierarchy in a classroom and a school rests on the perception that certain students are popular. Those popular students often hold the secrets and recognize the weaknesses of other children, and they use those secrets and weaknesses to control their peers. As one girl approaches the group she was included in yesterday, she is met with turned backs and whispered words shared by the few. In an effort to connect yesterday, she answered questions about herself, what boys and girls she liked, and those she didn't like. Today, those confidences and the efforts she made to be accepted are being used as weapons to hurt and humiliate her.

When you hear about kids being bullied at school or you see the videos of violence on school buses, you might be tempted to encourage your child to become almost invisible so as not to become a target. You might find yourself examining your child's behaviors and pointing out those that might be viewed as odd or nerdy. You could hear yourself saying things like, "Joey, your pants are pulled up too high," or "Don't tell the other kids that you still play dolls." The next thing you know, you have made your child so self-conscious that he or she can barely function in school.

In the average school setting, some kids are bullied regardless of what anyone does. If you think your child is being bullied, your first instinct might be to go after the bully—to go to school administrators or even the child's parents. Of course, if your child is being physically harmed or endangered, then you must first make sure she is safe. If that means keeping her out of school or having an immediate meeting with administrators to ensure that she is not harmed, then that's what you must do. If your child is not being physically harmed and she has not expressed suicidal or self-harming tendencies, then take a few minutes to consider your options. Decide where you can have the most significant and long-lasting impact. That is likely with your own child.

It is important to acknowledge the fear and pain that your child is experiencing when he is bullied. It is important to let him describe what is happening to him, by whom, and when it is happening. He needs to be able to tell you how he felt, what he did, and what he hopes will happen, knowing that you will not fall apart as he describes his tragic situation. Then, together, you can figure out what you can control.

Your child will likely beg you, "Please don't do anything. Please don't tell the principal." If that is what you have to do, then you want to let your child know early in the conversation that you will consider all options and that you will do whatever it takes to make sure he is safe. Don't lie and say you'll never go to school officials because you just might have to.

It is very unlikely that you can have any influence over the bully, who is often a child who has been bullied himself, and often in his own home. Many bullies live in chaotic or tense homes, and many are socially inept or feel incapable of managing their lives. They might struggle academically or appear to be athletically, physically, socially, and academically advanced. None of these characteristics is totally predictable. Essentially, a child who bullies is searching for a sense of control that comes from being in charge of the situation—regardless of his or her circumstances. You won't be able to directly address the needs or the actions of the bullying child, so focus your efforts on helping your own child manage his circumstances.

"Just ignore him; he'll quit and move on" doesn't work, and it diminishes the horror of the torment your child experiences. When you advise your child to remain silent in the face of bullying, you are essentially advising her to relinquish all power to the bully. Sadly, the message with this plan is that she is incapable of managing her day-to-day life. Your child may prefer this option because she is so fearful of the unknown results that will occur if she does something differently. The reality is that she's probably already hiding out and remaining mute, and she knows that this strategy hasn't worked. It even might have led to an escalation of the bullying. If, though, you can provide your child with a simple script—acknowledging that he hears the bully but that what is said is not affecting him—this might discourage further bullying behavior. A calm, logical, minimal response can discourage the bully when what she is seeking are tears and feelings of shame on the part of the victim. If a bully calls a child dumb, the victim can respond, "I'm not dumb enough to believe that." When a child is called fat or ugly, the victim can say, "I don't know. I think my weight is about right," or "I just look like an average kid." These reactions can be effective in discouraging the bully.

A young victim's dad or mom might decide to teach his victimized child how to fight the bully. Having seen this in the movies, the dad feels this is the answer to shutting up a mean kid. There is nothing wrong with teaching your child self-defense tactics, and if he feels more capable of managing a possible physical encounter, then he might be more able to shut the bully down using the previous verbal techniques. But encouraging your child to fight a boy who may well be the leader of a pack of boys or a boy who might just be twice his size may not be wise. Your son could land a punch and end up suspended from school for fighting. Yes, this might discourage others from bullying him, but it might not.

Emotions can run high when a child is bullied. She might feel angry, frustrated, sad, or humiliated. You will want to help your child develop strategies to manage her emotions in front of the bully. This doesn't mean, though, that she shouldn't express those emotions. She should be free to do that with you. Try to avoid the temptation to focus on the accuracy of the bully's comments with lines like, "But you're not fat!" or "You get better grades than he does!" The content of the comments, while terribly hurtful, are not really the point here. Your attempt to address them is futile. Let your child cry and rant and spill all the details. Steel yourself and provide the comfort she needs. Telling her not to cry or allowing her to cry in privacy will leave your child wondering if anyone really understands her situation. The goal here is to allow your child to express powerful feelings in a safe place and then to develop some good skills to control the emotions when she is with the bully.

Envisioning a shield can work. Your child can imagine that he has a shield he can bring down when the bully approaches. Then the cruel words bounce off the shield and right back to the speaker. If you can provide your child with a talisman, maybe a smooth stone or a seashell that he can keep in his pocket, he can rub the stone to remind himself to keep his emotions in check. There are many techniques that people use to recenter themselves and lower anxiety levels. You and your child need to find one that works and then practice it at home.

This is a grown-up problem. It is in these moments that adults must step in and save children from one another and from themselves. Sadly, many teachers and parents don't want to get mired in the relational dynamics of young adolescents. Either they remember all too well what the same experience was like for them, or they don't realize that there is a difference between getting involved in the mess and preventing the mess from happening.

While it may be uncomfortable for you to consider changing schools, there is a good possibility that the culture of your school is such that children are not expected to treat one another with respect and kindness. If in conversations with school administrators and teachers you encounter an attitude of benign neglect when it comes to bullying, then you should seriously consider changing schools. You do not want your child to spend eight hours a day, five days a week, for three years in a place where adults are not willing to protect children from themselves or one another. Reluctance to intervene can lead to catastrophic results. When young people feel that there is no acceptable way to escape the torment, they feel alone, unsupported, and unseen. They can see no way out.

WHEN YOUR CHILD IS A BULLY

What if you find out that your son is the bully? How can you help him to see the impact that his actions have on others? How do you convince him to care about the feelings of others? You need to find out what led to the bullying of this particular child. Was your son angry? Did he feel dismissed, or did he feel pressure to pick on this particular boy? Did the boy say something that embarrassed or hurt your son? Is your son being bullied himself, by either someone at school or someone in the family?

Regardless of the original incident that set off the bullying, if no one is bullying your child and she continues to victimize other children despite your discussions and warnings that there are consequences, then you will need to pursue two avenues simultaneously. You will need to make it clear once again that you believe that your child is a good person who has gone in the wrong direction and that this behavior is contrary to the values your family holds. This is one of those bad moments that must not be allowed to determine who your child is. After you have discussed the effects of bullying on others and some of the reasons that bullies bully, stop talking and move on. Certainly listen to her version of things, but don't be a fool.

One of the worst things a bully can say is, "I was only kidding." This is also one of the most common excuses kids who bully use to dismiss the child who reports his actions. This is not an acceptable excuse, because by now the bully knows that it can't be called kidding around if one person is terribly hurt by what is said and done. "He asked for it" or "She bullied me first" are not adequate excuses.

It's time to take action. First, make sure that your child knows that further bullying is unacceptable and it must stop immediately, no matter what. Then, find a way for your child to experience the feeling of doing something positive for someone else. Join him in volunteering for Habitat for Humanity or serving at a soup kitchen. Especially with boys, encourage them to think about the nature of honor and courage. Pull out the Douglas MacArthur quote:

> Duty, honor, country: Those three hallowed words reverently dictate what you ought to be, what you can be, what you will be. They are your rallying point to build courage when courage seems to fail, to regain faith when there seems to be little cause for faith, to create hope when hope becomes forlorn. They build your basic character. They mold you for your future roles as the custodians of the Nation's defense. They make you strong enough to know when you are weak, and brave enough to face yourself when you are afraid. They teach you to be proud and unbending in honest failure, but humble and gentle in success; not to substitute words for actions, not to seek the path of comfort, but to face the stress and spur of difficulty and challenge; to learn to stand up in the storm, but to have compassion on those who fall; to master yourself before you seek to master others; to have a heart that is clean, a goal that is high; to learn to laugh, yet never forget how to weep; to reach into the future, yet never neglect the past; to be serious, yet never to take yourself too seriously; to be modest so that you will remember the simplicity of true greatness, the open mind of true wisdom, the meekness of true strength.[1]

A lot of boy bullying is about proving manhood; it is a form of showman-ship meant to impress peers as much as it is aimed at the victim. MacArthur can introduce your son to a new version of manhood.

Second, encourage your child to stand up to problematic behavior. By standing up to those who talk about them or exclude them, your daughter can release her anger and frustration and move on. If she carries the anger and the slights around on their back, then sooner or later she will take them out on someone, most likely an innocent victim of her bullying.

Third, and most important, get your child to a good counselor or therapist. The longer you ignore or avoid this behavior, the harder it will be for your child to abandon it. If you don't address it, then eventually other kids will expect him to be a bully, and it will be almost impossible for him to change those expectations. Nice kids will pull away because they are wary that he will turn on them. He will find himself increasingly isolated by peers who are afraid of him, or he will find himself only associating with kids who are as mean or meaner than he is.

A counselor can work with your child to explore the reasons for the bully-ing and to find other ways to meet her need for control. This is one of those tough moments. No one wants to acknowledge that their child is unkind or disliked. You will automatically assume that somehow this is your fault—that something you said or did has permanently damaged your child's character. That is not productive.

Obviously, you want to get to the bottom of why she's bullying, and you may well hear that you will need to adjust some of the things you do and say. It does no good for your daughter, however, for you to carry the guilt for her sins. Unless you want her to grow into an adult bully, you need to face the facts and get her some help. This will let her know that you know she's a good person who has simply lost her way.

SEXUALITY IN MIDDLE SCHOOL

Kids are inundated with messages of overt sexuality from the time they are small. It's just that they are beginning to notice those messages and images when they reach middle school. Your children are fascinated and repulsed by their own and others' sexuality. That's okay.

Middle school–aged children need their questions about their bodies, sexu-ality, and even those huge questions about life and the world answered—by their parents. They need to know what's happening or will be happening to their bodies, and they need to know that every child grows up and changes on their own timetable. There are some great reference books out there that you can use to prepare yourself for conversations about puberty and sexuality.

You might be tempted to avoid embarrassment by just putting the book on your son's bed, but you know better.

Our society is oversexualized. Everywhere you look there are signs of this. Walk into the eatery at the local mall, and you will encounter people of all ages eating their lunch, socializing, and having a great time. Scattered throughout this wonderful socializing space are portable billboards with Victoria's Secret models in bras and panties. Stores selling women's underwear display mannequins in the window in thongs and garter belts.

Turn on any sports event on television and see commercials for medications that show naked women and men in bed barely under the covers. These scenes are so prevalent that they become hallmarks of society for your kids. They can start to believe that this is how they should behave, that this is the ideal. Marketing and advertising executives are stealing your child's childhood right in front of your eyes.

During these middle school years, you will need to come to grips with the idea that it's time to teach your child about the connection between love, relationships, and sexuality. They are desperate for information and at the same time might do anything they can to avoid the cringeworthy conversations that you seek to have with them. They are pretty sure that their friends can give them the capsulized version of the stuff they need to know. In order to ease embarrassment and discomfort, prepare yourself a script, study it, dig up some courage, and get to it!

Discussions of relationships and sexual activity are not the same as discussions of puberty. Prior to the relationship discussion, your son or daughter should be informed about the changes that are taking place or about to take place in their bodies. This is where a good book with diagrams in it can come in handy. You can't be expected to be completely informed about all the changes that are happening internally and externally, but you will want to inform yourself before you explain things to your child.

Once you have covered the physical and developmental aspects of puberty and adolescence, you will want to start the next crucial phase of discussions. Starting with some open-ended questions can help ease your way into the topic:

- "Have you ever thought about getting married someday?"
- "Did I ever tell you the story of how your dad and I met and fell in love?" (This one works well with girls.)
- "After we watched that movie last night, I wonder what your thoughts are on the relationship the two main characters had?"
- Or more directly, "I know there are some really nice girls in your class. Is there any one girl that you particularly like? Does she know it? How would you (could you) or (did you) let her know that you like her?"

General conversation starters might work:

- "What is a good age for kids to start dating?"
- "What does dating mean now?"
- "Can I tell you what it meant to be dating someone when I was a teenager?"

All of these are questions that might lead into the topic. They also might not work at all. Your other option is to charge right in.

In either case, the most important thing to do is to express your firm belief that there can be no separation between relationship and sexual activity. Simply insisting, "Don't consider having sex with someone unless you love them," will not be particularly effective. By introducing the topic of love and relationships, you can move more naturally into the topic of sexuality.

As the conversation progresses, you will want to know how much your son or daughter knows about sex or thinks they know:

- "Can you tell me what you know about the connection between a loving relationship and a sexual relationship?"
- "How much do you know about what it means to have sex?"

These questions may be met with silence or groans, but if you can sit in the quiet for a while, you will eventually get an answer of some kind.

Do boys have to have this talk with their dads? Should it only be Mom who talks to girls? If you are a single parent, you might be tempted to hand this off to someone else. Is that a good idea? The answers to these questions depend entirely on the comfort level of kids and parents and your ability to stay with the topic despite a little embarrassment. "The Talk" shouldn't take place all at once either. It should happen at opportune moments and should be temporarily suspended if it becomes overwhelming for your son or daughter or even for you! (Note the word *temporarily*.)

By now you have established a close relationship with your child, one that sets clear boundaries and assures your child that you are available to him when he needs you. This will allow you both to move through an uncomfortable talk and laugh a little, learn a little, and then move on to something else. Revisit the topic after something triggers it. A movie or television show, hearing something on the news, or just a few quiet moments in the car can set you up for a brief recap or some new information.

"THEY TAUGHT WHAT?"

Sexual education classes in school cover a wide range of topics. You will want to be thoroughly informed about what is being taught at school so that you can make a reasoned decision about whether you want your child to participate in those classes or so that you can follow up the classes with your own thoughts.

Some sexual education classes cover physical and emotional development exclusively. Some classes include discussions of gender identity issues at length and cover same-sex relationships and bisexuality, as well as transgender issues and binary sexuality. Some classes provide graphic details regarding sexual intercourse, oral sex, and anal sex.

It's important to ask questions of school administrators and teachers. Are the classes taught to single-sex groups, or does everyone hear the information at the same time in the same room? Do the talks cover the mechanics of sexual intercourse, the options for protection, same-sex activity, and other information that you may or may not want your child to hear?

You need to decide how and when you want your child to receive information about sexuality. You will need to talk with your spouse or, if you are a single parent, a trusted family member. Talk with your child to decide if he or she should cover this information with you or if you are comfortable with someone else presenting the information.

Depending on her level of maturity and comfort level, you might decide to provide your perspective on the topic, and then let your child attend the classes at school. You can also decide that this information is best shared within your home by you. This is important stuff. Take some time before you sign that permission slip. If there is no permission slip, then make sure that you know when, where, how, and by whom the classes are scheduled to be taught.

This is not a decision to be made based on what your friends think or because you don't want the teachers to be upset with you. This is an incredibly personal topic, and the decision should be a personal one, based on the answers you receive from teachers and administrators, your knowledge of your child, and your family values.

Your child deserves to have information about puberty and sexuality. It would be a mistake to decide that the topic is best left alone. You will then have no control over what she learns.

The Wilsons

The Wilsons were a family of six: two parents, two boys, and two girls. Every summer, they spent time at the beach, a three-hour drive away. Some of the children would ride with their dad, and some would ride with their mom. Mom ensured that one of the children rode with her when it was time, the first time in the summer before sixth grade, then again before ninth grade, and at least once or twice in between.

The boys especially tried to avoid riding with Mom because they knew she would be talking about something uncomfortable, but they also laughed about it, considering it a rite of passage. She knew that it was much easier for them to hear what she was saying if she wasn't sitting right across from them. They could look out the car window, grunting or nodding every once in a while to let her know they were listening. After she'd had her say, they'd stop for ice cream or turn up the radio and enjoy the rest of the ride.

The kids needed more than those talks, though. They learned from their father how a good man treats the women in his life and from their mother how a woman treats the men in her life. They needed to know how a boy should treat his sister, his mother, his classmates, a girl he likes, and a girl who gets on his last nerve. They needed to know that a girl's sense of humor, kindness, and intelligence will make her attractive. A word of advice: These conversations can be easier if they are combined with a physical chore or exercise of some kind.

BEING NICE

The simplest message is the most effective. When your son has made someone cry or when your daughter has been rude or disrespectful, the message can be concise: "If you want people, girls or boys or grown-ups, to like you, just be nice, polite, and respectful." It is straightforward and simple, and it is right. When your children focus their energy on being nice, their level of comfort with their classmates and with themselves improves. Reminders are easy; teachers and parents can simply say, "Remember to be nice."

The rules are clear, and they always apply. Speak and act respectfully toward adults and peers; protect your siblings at all costs; include others; and never disrespect, take advantage of, or mistreat another person—boy or girl—whether you like the person or not.

OPPORTUNITIES FOR ADVENTURE

"The Last of the Monsters with Iron Teeth" tells the story of a band of hundreds of children who came to believe that there was a vampire with iron teeth who had killed and eaten "two wee boys" in Glasgow.[2] The children banded together and stormed a local cemetery, hunting for the vampire. This hunt turned out to be one of many monster hunts that occurred in Glasgow and across the United Kingdom, some of which lasted several nights.

While no one—well, except the children involved—would encourage children today to go monster hunting in large groups, there is something very appealing about a gang of children latching on to a tale of monsters and banding together to fight the boogeymen. Their hunting expedition would likely be their first experience with the spirit of group courage that arises from pursuing a common cause.

Children no longer have much opportunity to roam our towns and neighborhoods, creating stories, chasing imagined demons, and testing their courage. Anxious parents don't think that they can trust people in the greater community not to harm their children. They don't even trust that the neighbors will keep an eye out for their wandering children. So children are confined to their own backyards or a rented field where they are closely supervised by coaches and parents. Every once in a while, a small tribe might find a way to escape, and have an adventure all on their own, surely an adventure they will not forget.

BOY TRIBES

Michael Gurian in *The Wonder of Boys* articulates a belief that boys need a tribe.[3] Most boys can find their primary tribe in their own family, where they know that, no matter what, they need to watch out for one another. In family, they are their true selves with one another. They learn to negotiate, to cheat one another, and to experience guilt. They learn to keep secrets from their parents for the good of all, and they learn to slide down the steps in sleeping bags without smashing into the living room furniture.

They need to be told often, "Your friends will come and go, but your brothers and sisters will always be there for you." If you want that to be true and you reinforce the message regularly, then it will become reality. They can create other tribes, too—in their schools, sports teams, bands, clubs, and neighborhood crew. Within those tribes, they find shared purpose and hours of shared fun.

While in middle school, most boys are in same-sex tribes. They may be very aware of the girls but not yet mature enough to establish or maintain meaningful friendships with girls because they risk ostracism, teasing, or rejection if they try. The different tribes to which a boy belongs can have an impact on the way he treats other people. Middle school boys are somewhat adrift. They aren't sure who they want to be or even who they are right this minute.

If he is in the outcast tribe—the boys who are not accepted to the group at the top of the hierarchy or even the group in the middle of the hierarchy—then he is at something of an advantage. He doesn't have lots of popular friends, but he just needs a small group of friends. He can take his time growing up and establishing his identity because no one is expecting him to set the pace or be a trendsetter.

The boys at the top of the heap may be at a disadvantage, however. They are seen as leaders and guys who know about all the stuff guys should know. They are likely more popular with the girls because they are not as intimidated by them and know how to talk with them. They are often expected to mimic the teens who are in high school, and they are expected to be cool and unaffected by most things most of the time. They are almost stuck in the role of cool, even when they don't really have any idea who or how they want to be.

If your boy is part of the large group in the middle, the group that is moving its way toward the top but will certainly thin out before it gets there, then he will either need to be aware and ready to move up at all times, or he can settle himself into either of the lower groups and be content with having all kinds of friends and staying true to himself, his interests, and his values. This will provide him with the time and opportunity to determine who and how he will be.

You want to know who is in your boy's tribe. The people with whom he spends his time will influence the way he talks, dresses, acts, and thinks. The desire to fit in and be accepted is a powerful force. If his tribe is dominated by boys who are determined to break all the rules or boys who are unkind, then he will eventually come to follow their lead if he wants to remain connected. Are your son's friends helping him become his best self? Are they developing a sense of camaraderie that is based on adventure and fun, or are they pulling him down? If you're not sure, then find out. It's a mistake, though, to limit your boy's tribe to children who look and live just like he does. Outliers can create a lot of excitement and some great experiences for the boys in the tribe.

Invite boys to come to your house when you're around. Food is always a draw. Make sure you have cookies and pizza and lots of snacks around. You don't have to interview them or sit in the room with them. Just listen and watch what you can watch. You'll be able to recognize the good kids, and you'll get a sense of the boys who might pose some risks. If you have concerns, carefully voice them to your son: "Tell me more about Hank. He seems very different from your other friends. Is he a good friend?" If you've taught your son to include the guy who is excluded, you might be seeing that in action with Hank. Trust your instincts. If it looks like these boys are creating a bond, looking out for one another, and having fun, then let them!

GIRL TRIBES

Girls need a female tribe. Girls need at least one or two friends that they can count on. Other friends will come and go as the ever-changing dynamics of middle school girl friendships change. They need to learn from the women in their lives how to treat other girls, how to laugh at things that only girls and women think are funny, and how to subtly indicate spinach in teeth and hair that needs combing. Girls need to connect with their family history by hearing their mothers', aunts', and grandmothers' stories.

They need to understand the important, sometimes unrecognized contributions their female relatives have made to the sustenance of the family over time. This is how girls learn to be strong women of character and kindness. Girls need mothers, aunts, grandmothers, and other adult women around them. The women in your daughter's life can share great stories and give great advice that will help her to figure her own way through the challenges of middle school.

Your child's safety has always been a priority to you, and it will remain that way as she enters adolescence and beyond. You want to be sure to safeguard your child's physical health, but just as important right now is her heart and soul. Girls need to hear, more than a few times, that their value lies not in their looks or their ability to attract attention but in their character. This counter-cultural message can easily be drowned out by what is all around girls—on social media, on Netflix and weekly TV sitcoms, in commercials and print advertisements, and of course even in the hallways of her school or down the street. So it's up to you to speak up and speak often. No girl deserves to be diminished by believing that she is only as good as her body.

GIRLS USING WORDS

When do things get flipped upside down and backward? When is it that girls stop speaking out and speaking up? When do they decide that it's easier or more effective to go around and through the back door rather than charging right through the front? How many times do teachers and mothers tell little girls to be nice or lower their voices? How often are girls praised in school for having nice handwriting or neat uniforms while their male counterparts are praised for being first, being strong, or having good ideas? It happens right here in middle school. The groundwork is laid early, but during middle school, we see the effects of the messages they have received over the years.

If girls still have recess, they might spend their time huddled in small groups on the perimeter of the playground. They believe that their power rests in their ability to use language to control their situations. Girls who don't fit a certain mold can be ostracized. Boys can be used as an indicator of one's power. So while girls' voices might have been quieted in the larger world, they find a way to use their words to maintain some control over their lives within the hallways of their schools and in their homes.

Unless strong teachers and vigilant parents recognize what is happening, these young girls can become mean girls or mean girls' victims in no time at all. Unchecked, two or three girls can affect the lives of every girl and boy in their class—and change the course of their development.

LEARNING TO MANAGE CONFLICT

While it may seem counterintuitive, the last thing you want to do is protect your child from conflict. Consider that you want your son or daughter to know how to handle conflict, how to think under pressure, and how to avoid resorting to emotional outbursts to escape difficult intellectual or performance challenges.

It's up to you to teach your children to channel powerful emotions and combine them with their equally powerful intellect. If they learn to do this, then they will soon be able to create reasonable responses in conflict situations. Practice, rehearse scenarios, and encourage your adolescent to continue to inform himself about issues that come up.

RISK TAKING

Risk taking is part and parcel of an adolescent's life. Adolescents should be encouraged to dream big and think big. It can be difficult to let your son or daughter pursue the monsters if you are an anxious parent. Be sure that your first response to a potential adventure isn't always "No." Try to envision the glitter in your son's adventure. Focus on the shiny part of watching your boy grow by stretching himself beyond what he thinks he can do.

During the early adolescence years, children tend to take low to moderate risks, like going beyond the boundaries their parents have set for them to travel alone or in a pack of friends. They can learn a lot from those excursions, and if you have regulated and controlled all their "free" time with organized, adult-supervised activities, they need to break out once in a while.

Children at this age might push the limits at school. Mostly just to see what happens, they might skip school or part of the school day when they realize that no one will notice. They aren't driving, so they can't go far or do much, but the idea of unsanctioned freedom can be very appealing.

This is also when they might try shoplifting, especially if the children in their tribe encourage the practice. You will need to talk to your children about acceptable risks and provide them opportunities to engage in appropriate risk-taking behavior—like riding terrifying roller coasters, white water rafting with Dad, playing hide-and-seek on a Saturday night with friends, or camping under the stars.

When your child takes a risk that clearly jeopardizes his or her safety, disobeys a rule at school, or breaks the law, then the consequences need to be swift and unequivocal. Children need to know that they may not, under any circumstance, endanger their own health or lives or violate the trust of teachers or parents.

Before you decide on the safety issue, though, step back and carefully consider their need for unregulated time to explore the world. Have you controlled your child's life and activities so much that he feels compelled to break the rules just to have some fun? Are you overreacting to natural behaviors? Is the danger you see real or imagined? Is it bloody-knee danger or broken-neck, go-to-jail danger?

BEING THE BIGGEST FAN

Even as your tween begins to establish herself as an independent young person, she still needs to know that you are her biggest fan and strongest supporter. It is important to remind him regularly that you trust him to do the right thing and to manage most of the challenges he faces. Promise her you will always be there when she needs a helping hand or someone to lean on. Then keep your promise.

Chapter 10

School Life of Tweens,
Ages Ten to Fourteen

TIME MANAGEMENT AND ORGANIZATION

There is a huge amount of learning going on for children in middle school—
and the essentials of school often get in the way of that learning. Homework,
teachers insisting on teaching prealgebra or American history, papers to be
written, and math homework *every single night* can all interfere with the
social life your middle schooler is building. Your children will begin to recognize the need for organization and time-management skills. After-school
activities may run until 8:00 or 9:00. This means, of course, that homework
will need to fit into the schedule at some point. Middle schoolers are developing physically, and they need to get a good night's sleep. Putting homework off until after play practice or the basketball scrimmage minimizes the
importance of homework. Once they are in middle school, students will have
more homework, and they will need to study for frequent and more difficult
assessments.

This is a time to be especially organized yourself. If you can demonstrate
calm and patient planning, then your child will be able to ask for your help
when she needs it. In the beginning of the school year, she may need your
help as she prioritizes homework assignments.

Some students prefer to attack the hardest subjects first and move on to the
easier assignments when that is done. Others prefer to get the easy stuff out of
the way before tackling a challenging assignment. Give your child the opportunity to try each approach a few times, and then encourage him to settle on
one and stick with it. It is important for a parent to be nearby, available to talk
things through in the beginning. A good start will make all the difference as
the difficulty level increases.

Children should have a quiet space within which to work. They should have the necessary supplies and a scheduled time for homework. That scheduled time may have to be different every night due to after-school activities. This is where a clear and color-coded calendar and an extra set of textbooks kept at home will come in handy. It can be hard to remember what's due when and what homework must be done when one is occupied with other responsibilities and preoccupied with his social life.

During designated homework time, cell phones should be out of reach. Use of the computer for anything other than schoolwork should be prohibited. These restrictions may seem unreasonable to your child, but they will give her the time and the space to complete her homework.

Many children will benefit from the use of speech-to-text options on their computers for writing assignments. This allows them to get their thoughts out quickly so that they can then go back and organize and edit their ideas.

AVOIDING THE MATH MYTH

It is often the case in middle school that girls decide they can't do math. If a girl has become a good reader, then she will likely love the language arts and any assignment that requires her to express herself in writing. It may well take her longer to complete math problems because girls tend to consider all the options and alternatives, but math is looking for one specific answer. It is important for you to encourage your daughter to work on her math skills and to consider the value they will bring to her in the future.

Work with her to figure out her grade point average at the end of each quarter and to consider how it would change if certain grades go up or down next quarter. Ask her to help you bake or cook, and consider taking a sewing class together. If she likes sports, then figure out batting averages, average points per game, average times in track meets, or the likelihood that a team will win based on their and their opponents' win-loss record.

Middle school girls are already considering possible career paths, and as your daughter does this, it is important to discuss with her where math comes into play, whether she wants to be a doctor, a designer, an engineer, or even a teacher.

THE NEED FOR MOVEMENT AND CHOICE

School is not necessarily a friendly place for middle school boys. Teachers may find it difficult to tolerate boys' need to move frequently. Classrooms are largely organized for sedentary reception of information from the authority figure in the room. Boys generally do well when they can engage with the material in a physical way, when they can make choices, and when they feel valued. All students are far more likely to remember the history lesson if they are given a chance to create a huge timeline on the floor with drawing paper and markers. They experience and then remember how to find area, circumference, and more when they are allowed to measure objects in the building or on the playground with tape measures and yardsticks. Percentages are best learned when they can use sports team statistics or grades—particularly their own.

READING THE CUES

If teachers complain that your child doesn't listen and follow directions the first time, then it is likely that she is not paying attention. It may happen that everyone is sitting in their seats, ready to begin a lesson, and your child is still chatting with a friend. Teachers can interpret this behavior as willful disobedience when it is an attention issue. Work with the teacher. Find out how she indicates that students should listen or sit or line up. Practice with your child at home.

For some children, these are skills that they do not have naturally. If you think a keyword from the teacher will work to grab your child's attention, then ask the teacher if she can use the keyword to see if that helps. Some children need a visual cue, like a tap on the desk or just eye contact with the teacher. If the teacher wants your child to pay attention and participate in class, then she will be willing to add these small touches to her instructional techniques.

HOLDING HIGH STANDARDS

During the middle school years, the perception that boys who are good students are nerds can rear its ugly head. It is important to stress high standards in all areas—sports, extracurriculars, behavior, and academics for boys who begin to think it's not cool to be a good student. At the same time, many middle school girls restrict their participation in classes for fear of being seen as stupid or as the teacher's pet. They will do well to remember that their participation and their questions can clarify information for them and for other students who might feel too shy to ask questions.

ACADEMIC STRUGGLES

When their sons or daughters get poor grades, many parents consider withdrawing their child from sports teams or other activities. Thinking that this will force the child to study more and get better grades, they limit their child's life to school, homework, and nothing else. In fact, girls and boys who are involved in sports, dance, clubs, or other activities tend to learn to manage their time better than those who go to school, come home, and have hours to kill before bedtime.

If your son or daughter is struggling academically, you will first need to understand why. Is it because he's hearing that it's not cool to be smart? Is it because she really hasn't figured out how to prioritize and manage her time? Is it because your 9:00 p.m. bedtime doesn't afford him the time to complete his homework? Or is it because she spends her homework time texting or looking at Instagram?

The only way to answer these questions is to talk to your child, watch them, talk to teachers, and listen to him and his friends when they are together. Once you know what the problem is, you can address it appropriately. You can remove the phone or the laptop from his room. You can spend a *brief* time talking about how much you value academic work and even more time listening to him talk about school and what his solutions might be for the homework problem.

You can get her some additional academic support if she needs it. You can let her stay up until 10:00 if she agrees to complete all her schoolwork each night. You can also check her homework organizer and her work every night, and that might be necessary for a while. The trouble is that this solution will not make her more accountable. It will just make you accountable for checking and making sure she does what she's supposed to.

IN THE CLASSROOM

Self-confidence can fade quickly when boys and girls are in middle school. A girl might sit quietly through class after class, staring at her fingernails or looking out the window. She will do anything to avoid being called on or singled out. She wants to avoid being seen as too smart, silly, or stupid at all costs. She might also dread being seen as a teacher's pet. What a balance children must keep! Teachers tend to call on boys more often than girls, and boys tend to call out, often stifling quieter students' desire to contribute during class.

It is important to ask your children about their teachers and classes. Specifically ask, "Tell me how Dr. Rogers runs his class. Do you get to contribute, or is it mostly a lecture?" Ask about which teachers want to hear from everyone. Ask them about their favorite subjects and classes and why they like them. Ask them about their least favorite classes and why.

But wait! If you ask all these questions at once, your child will suspect that you're up to something. He might be afraid to answer your questions, especially if he thinks you're going to complain about a teacher at school. He might also worry that you will gossip about what he tells you. Reassure your child that you hold your conversations with him to be private, and you would never gossip about what you talk about with him.

You might hear that the teacher lets kids yell out or talk during class. You might hear that the teacher embarrasses kids when they get the answer wrong or if they say they don't know. This can lead to a larger and more practical discussion. Neither you nor your child can effect change in every teacher or class, but you can counter the impact a poor teacher has on your child by showing her what it looks like to have and share an opinion. You can talk to her about what it's like to deal with someone who is attempting to ignore or dismiss you and what it's like to be assertive and not shrill, angry, or whiny. Share examples from your younger years and even examples from your current work. You want your child to know that being a victim will not serve her well, and that she won't easily change other people. She can, though, learn to assert herself without being obnoxious or rude. One of the most important lessons children can learn from having teachers they don't really like is how to work with, learn from, and create some kind of relationship with people about whom they can't find much to like.

As they progress through middle school, children should be celebrated for their academic victories and held accountable for the work they are expected to do at school. Setting reasonable limits on activities and outings that interfere with homework and family time can be challenging, but it is necessary. Kids in middle school are still children and are not always able to balance these demands on their own. With parental guidance and direction, boys and girls who are engaged in extracurricular activities during the school year can become adept at time management and prioritizing—two skills they will need as they enter high school.

INDEPENDENCE VERSUS IMMATURITY

This is a time when struggles and conflicts will arise as your child's need to be independent bumps up against her inability to manage her increasing responsibilities in the academic arena. You will need patience, flexibility, determination, and creativity to help your child become a good student and a responsible young person.

Chapter 11

Family Life of Teenagers

STAYING IN THE GAME

Once they are in high school, teenagers have far less contact with their parents. When overscheduled parents try to grab five minutes here or there, their efforts are often met with silence or a one- or two-word response and then an escape. Teenagers, like most of us, don't share under pressure or on demand. They share in spurts and at moments of their choosing. You need to be ready to listen. You need to be willing to put down what you're doing, even if it's a work call or an important email. Stopping in your teen's room before bedtime can provide an opening for him after he's had time to consider how his day went.

When your teenager complains that you're the only parent who calls ahead when he goes to a party at a friend's house or that he's the only kid who can't hang out at the mall on Saturday evening, remind him that having a weird parent builds character. This can help him if he finds himself trying to avoid a troublesome situation. He can always blame his "ridiculously overprotective parent/parents" when he decides to pass on risky behavior.

THE BALANCE BETWEEN INDEPENDENCE
AND FAMILY TIES

It can be challenging to balance the teenager's need for independence and continued accountability for her behavior. It may feel like much of this is a guessing game, but you know your children. If your instinct tells you that something is too risky, then it most likely is! Trust your instincts but know the difference between instincts and fears. If you operate from a place of fear when it comes to your children, you will find yourself limiting too much.

Teenagers are resourceful, and they are adept at developing ways to experience some things despite your best efforts. If you've used every opportunity to listen and to talk with your child, then you can be pretty sure he will hear your voice in his head when he goes somewhere or does something you don't approve. That might keep him from doing anything really stupid or dangerous.

You still have opportunities to reinforce the lessons you've been teaching since he was little. You just have to be more subtle, and you have to pick your moments carefully. Objectifying lessons can help. Seeking his opinions on relationships or situations that are portrayed on television or on current news stories will allow your teen to consider how today's societal standards correspond to what he has been taught about how the world works and the values he holds.

Look for opportunities to volunteer at school dances when your children are in high school. Often, parent chaperones are reluctant to intervene when young people are acting inappropriately. Chaperones are there to save young people from themselves and to provide them with a safety net so that things do not get out of control, so take your job seriously! Just as you had to tell your kids to stop picking their noses or grabbing toys from their friends, you might have to tell teens to stop twerking or stop putting their hands on other young people who do not welcome their advances. Just as you taught your daughters not to sit with their legs wide open when wearing a skirt, it is your job to tell them when their top is cut too low or that their underpants show when they bend over in a miniskirt.

Once children reach their teen years, the adults around them seem to abandon common sense. Fully grown adults can suddenly become shy about parenting, reluctant to say no, deferring to the judgment of sixteen-year-olds. Is it possible that, once kids look like adults, their parents think their work is done?

TEENAGE GIRLS

Teenage girls can be incredibly challenging and difficult. They are also a lot of fun to be around. They run fast and furious or so slow as to appear comatose. They express themselves in traditional ways—with tears, stomping feet, squeal-filled hugs, and loud laughter. Or they suppress their emotions, appearing uncaring, aloof, angry, quiet, or stoic. Each of them is different, of course, and each of them can be all these things at one time or another.

Parents need to remain close but not too close. You cannot face the challenges your daughter faces, but you can remain vigilant and available and provide your girl with a sounding board and frequent opportunities to talk through her dilemmas.

Recent data released by the US surgeon general reveals the frightening hazards faced by teenage girls. One in five girls report having experienced sexual violence in the past year, and one in ten girls report that she has been forced to have sex in the last year, so it is no wonder that our girls are suffering.[1]

TEENAGE BOYS

While they will certainly be the cause of some parental gray hair, teenage boys can also be funny, affectionate, thoughtful, and creative. They bring you shiny moments—like when they help their grandmother out to her car and when they pop in with a spontaneous hug. They enjoy being responsible and accomplishing tasks. The confidence they gain by facing difficult choices and choosing correctly will be a valuable trait as they get older. They need to be given important work to do at home and in the larger world.

DANGEROUS TIMES

Sons and daughters are in danger of being disconnected from their parents. That attachment that you worked so hard to establish when they were babies, those hours you spent reading, teaching, and playing with your children, are being challenged by the messages of a culture that espouses values completely contrary to those you hold dear. Predators enter their lives easily and constantly via social media. TikTok, Instagram, and other social media sites are doing their best to steal your girls and your boys from you, convincing them that they are worthless.

As your child enters her teens, it is far more important for you to listen more than you talk. Once you have made your values and expectations clear in those small and big moments of growing up, it's time to let your child determine what she believes—about herself and about how she wants to relate to other people. You can listen, and you can encourage her to protect herself from being denigrated and diminished.

In almost all cases, children are not destined to become difficult teenagers. It is not inevitable that your teen will stop speaking to you—or that he will speak to you with obvious disdain, in a condescending and disrespectful tone. It is not written in the stars that teens will lock themselves in their rooms for hours, even days, without ever acknowledging the existence of their family members. Regardless of what you read, all teenagers do not take drugs, binge drink, hate their parents, or have sex in the school hallways.

While teenagers are navigating the unknown terrain between childhood and adulthood, they can experience moodiness, sadness, depression, and a desperate desire to be independent. They can have an equally desperate need to remain connected to their families—all at the same time. If their feet are firmly planted in a strong sense of belonging and accountability to their family, and if they know that their parents trust them conditionally and love them unconditionally, then the whole family is more likely to weather the teenage years and maybe even enjoy them.

If, however, somewhere along the line, your daughter has come to think that you are the enemy or that she is the most important person in the universe and everyone exists to serve, then you've got trouble. In many families, the teenagers run the show, and the parents are whirling from one crisis to another, always left waiting and wondering just outside the door.

CONTRIBUTING

Reminding teens that they are needed and that they have a responsibility to contribute at home, at school, and in their community can help them to develop habits of excellence:

PARENT: I need you to take the trash out before you leave. *This communicates that this is not just something you want him to do. It's something you need him to do.*

TERRY: Sorry, Joe's outside. I have to go.

PARENT: Take the trash out first, please. Joe will wait for you. *You both know Joe's not going to drive off without him, and you are respectfully reminding him to be respectful.*

Less nagging; fewer "or elses"; and more consistency, clarity of expectations, and face-to-face conversations all can help when reminding teens to do their part and helping them to remain respectful.

As your teen gets older, it can be productive to articulate the many tasks involved in keeping the family home operating. Then you can give him some choices. Let him identify the additional tasks that he will take on. Giving a teen a grocery list while you run other errands allows her to rehearse adulthood and maybe get a few things for herself. She may not do a perfect job getting the items you want, and she might even pack the bag with the bread under the giant container of sour cream, but she will figure things out eventually.

It may feel pretty good when your teenager gets his driver's license. You've been waiting for someone to help you with carpooling and errands. Your teenager might be eager to get out of the house by himself. Don't be surprised, though, when the keys get lost and you get a call late at night to pick him up. You may not feel all that patient or understanding, but because you know it's a likely occurrence, you won't be caught completely unaware. Teenagers get distracted and they misplace things, especially when they are excited. Once he has to spend several hours the next day getting a new set of keys made and buying a great big key chain, he will learn his lesson.

Sending your teen to drop off a package at the post office or to the dry cleaners gives her a chance to drive around with a purpose. Be sure you let her know, though, when you expect her home. Allow fifteen to thirty minutes extra for her to stop at McDonald's or to get lost on the way.

UNTIL THE LAST WHISTLE

When parents shrug their shoulders and comment, "Just trying to survive until he goes to college," or, "Our kids spend all their time on their devices. They never want to talk to us," common sense has been abandoned. "Kids are going to drink and try drugs. We should at least make sure they're safe and let them do it at home," or, "Get her the pill now to avoid a tragedy later," can be some of the most dangerous things parents say. Teenagers still need guidance, even if they don't want to hear it.

Some parents come to the tragic conclusion that they don't much like their teenagers and their teenagers don't like much about them. If this is the case for you, take some time to ask yourself why this young person you love so much is not particularly likable right now. Can you acknowledge a couple things? First, you have probably played a big part in creating this ungrateful young person, and second, that it's not too late to do something about that!

It can help to look back at what has been communicated to kids so that mistakes can be acknowledged and learned from. Then, everyone can move on. If parents pretend that they haven't created the entitled, indulged, anxious, unhappy children they have living in their houses, then there is no way they can change things when they recognize the need to do something.

PLEASING OTHERS

Teenagers who cheat on tests; break into tears or fury when they get a B on an assignment; self-medicate anxiety with alcohol, drugs, or food; or find it almost impossible to relax and have fun are most often driven by a belief that they need to be perfect. They feel certain that they are loved because they accomplish, because they do everything well. They are driven to make the adults in their lives proud and to ensure that those adults will love them. They don't come up with these ideas on their own.

This can happen when adults fail to work through the process of parenting with their kids. Instead, they decide early on that they will produce the child every parent wants: the straight-A student who gets into a great high school, stars on the football team, gets a scholarship to college, and goes to medical school. They are convinced that this success will make their children into happy adults, and they love their children so much that they want them to be happy always.

In this scenario, what the adults miss is what's happening right in front of them. They don't see the glitter, the shiny moments of silly creative fun, or the difficult moments that forge strong character and resilience in their children. Instead, everything must be a step toward the goal. Nothing is appreciated for what it is right now. When things go wrong, they must be fixed immediately, or they will derail this train to success.

When these children get caught cheating or ticketed for underage drinking, their parents' first thought might be, "Everyone will know. This is mortifying." These parents will call a friend or the friend of a friend to get the situation taken care of before any consequences must be paid. Consequently, their children's growing up becomes all about the adults who can brag about their achievements, adults who will fix things, adults who don't believe that their kids can grow up without interference.

These young people struggle to live with the enormous responsibility they feel to accomplish what their parents want. A sense that they aren't really in charge of their lives combines with a belief that they will never be held accountable for their behavior. This makes for a lot of confusion and a lack of personal direction. Eventually these young people can come to believe that they are victims—of others who have more, of parents who want more, of those who get the promotion they wanted, of life itself. They can come to believe that they are incapable of effecting change in their own lives.

WHAT ARE THEY DOING?

There are some teenagers who seem hell-bent on destruction, usually their own. They seem to sabotage every opportunity they are given. They might look like they're focused solely on having fun and breaking all the rules, but what is really going on? What picture of life do they have? Are they just searching for a way to get their parents to step in and parent them? Are they desperate for someone to set some limits for them, someone to hold them accountable, someone to notice? Have they been introduced to the idea that they are here for a greater purpose, not just fun or chaos? Or are they fighting back against unreasonable limits, expectations, and restrictions that don't allow them any sense of independence?

The point is not to blame parents for the choices their teenagers make. Teenagers are old enough and informed enough to make decisions about how they will manage the gift of life they have been given, and blaming parents for their poor decisions just validates the view that teenagers are not accountable for anything. However, parents might need to acknowledge their role in the current predicament and in the fact that their teen either feels entitled to break the rules or has chosen poorly. Painful as that might be, it is a necessary step toward a solution to the current catastrophe.

MAKING YOUR OWN LUCK

Everyone knows one of those families where the kids seem to always do the right thing. They show up at school and work hard. They're respectful to teachers and kind to friends. Well-behaved children who manage to avoid trouble most of the time is the result of hard work. When they take a wrong turn, the adults in their lives don't waste a lot of time considering options. There are consequences to be paid for behaviors that put them or someone else in danger. Car keys taken away, privileges suspended, apology letters written—all these "old-fashioned consequences" are used to remind children that they are better than their mistakes and that parents can be trusted to address those mistakes in a way that allows their child a chance to recover, regroup, and then get back to life.

It doesn't pay to compare your child to those other seemingly perfect children. No one can see clearly what happens in another family home. Each family is unique, and each child is a favorite child to his parents. Each child has her own mission on this earth, and it's your job to help your children discover their calling, their purpose.

The idea that children have to live in this world—a world that is often hostile to their souls and their hearts—can be terrifying. That doesn't mean, though, that you have to buy into a society that does not value innocence, faith, or good behavior, nor should you tuck your child away from the world. Children, especially teenagers, are meant to be of this world, to contribute, and now is the time to convince them that they are capable of holding on against the tide. Now is the time to help them discover the strength and character that they have been building for the last sixteen years.

You don't want to relinquish your responsibilities when the challenges seem too great because your child is watching, and he will follow your lead. It is your job to fight for him all the way to adulthood.

NOT YOUR TEENAGER'S FRIEND

Your teen needs you to be an adult. She doesn't need a fifty-year-old friend. Your attempts to establish a close relationship with her can lead you to believe mistakenly that the best way to support her is to become her friend and confidant.

Growing up is her job. You will sometimes find yourselves caught between societal demands to cram life down her throat and the temptation to protect her from increasing responsibilities. Somewhere in the middle of the two is the sweet spot—finding it and holding it can be tough.

In order to effectively support your teenager as she grows up, you will need to establish reasonable boundaries and definitions for childhood and adulthood and then communicate that information with clarity and consistency. It's not fair to abandon your responsibilities because you need your teenager to like you. There will be times when she doesn't like you, but if you need to be admired, then find some adults to fill that need for you.

Teenagers need to know that the adults in their lives will help them by setting limits. They need to know that you don't expect them to agree with every decision you make, and that's okay. They also need to know that they are expected to follow the rules. You will save your teen a lot of heartache by giving him a curfew, controlling his phone and internet access, and talking to him about why adults can drink alcohol or smoke pot (although some shouldn't) and why kids cannot.

Human brains are not fully grown until they reach their late twenties. It's not fair to ask teenagers to make decisions they are ill-equipped to make. Instead, why not provide your daughter with the perfect excuse for missed parties or beach trips by being the "nutty, overprotective" parent? She will be sad to miss some of the fun, but she will not regret missing the drunken, drugged, or destructive behavior that often occurs. Teenagers need to know that their parents are determined to do whatever it takes to raise them with values and to help them to become productive citizens who will make the world a better place.

PROVIDING ALTERNATIVES AND
STAYING INVOLVED

Give your teen something meaningful to do and expect him to do it. Volunteer to coach a team with him, to paint a house, or to serve meals at a soup kitchen. Make sure he has obligations to a team, a club, the band, and other people.

Expect and encourage him to meet his obligations. Don't let him quit because things are hard.

If at all possible, be home when your teenager is home. If you can't be home when your teen is home, then make liberal use of FaceTime, or help your teen find an after-school job.

When you are home, put your phone down and turn the television off when she comes into the room. Watch her favorite show with her—without judging. Be ready to listen and avoid the impulse to tell her how to solve every problem she faces. Listen, reflect what you hear, ask what she thinks, and let her know you have faith in her ability to make the right decisions and do the right thing.

Ask your teen to explain how Instagram and TikTok work. Ask him the pros and cons of different sites and apps. By suspending judgment and asking him to explain the value of social media, you allow him to share what he knows and what he has experienced in those uncharted waters. Acknowledge that these are part of teenagers' lives but try to balance that with a discussion (not a lecture) about the downsides. You can ask,

- "Do a million likes convince a boy to like himself?"
- "Does sarcasm or teasing do damage when it occurs in text?"
- "Does an Instagram post really disappear?"
- "Does the iPhone get in the way of honest, face-to-face conversation with friends or family?"

Ask your teenager to consider a family ban on devices at the dinner table. Ask her what would likely happen if you tried it. Ask her who would have the most trouble with that restriction. Her answers might surprise you. She might even point out how often you disconnect from your family by picking up your phone.

With love, consistency, and a willingness to listen to your teenager as much as you talk, you can provide him with appropriate opportunities to develop independence and make reasoned decisions. These are essential skills that he will need when he is ready to leave the parental safety net behind.

YOUR TEEN'S JOB

Teenagers are supposed to challenge the adults in their lives. That's how they find out where the people they trust stand and how firmly they stand there, so you had better be ready to explain and, even more important, live by your professed values. Your child will be able to see through any contradictions quickly because she is watching, listening, and judging to figure out who you really are and who she will become. It's also important that parents iron out their own differences before their teen challenges their beliefs. Again, she will be able to tell when the people in charge aren't on the same page.

Fiery dinner-table conversations may not be the best thing for your digestion, but allowing for a discussion that entertains different points of view can be enormously good for a family. As long as everyone has the right to express their opinions without being silenced or ridiculed, you can learn a lot about how kids think and how the adults in their lives come across to them.

NOT WHAT IT LOOKS LIKE

Most healthy teenagers are focused on just a few things:

- To keep some part of their lives to themselves
- To get around rules they consider too restrictive
- To create an identity for themselves
- To have that identity validated by those around them
- To establish and maintain connections with other people
- To be committed to social justice

What looks like sneakiness or dishonesty simply might be your teen's way of creating some sense of privacy. You don't need all the details of your teenager's life. Far better to ask one or two open-ended questions and then listen!

When you see what looks like your teen desperately searching for a way to escape from home, she might simply be asking for time each day to be in the world, able to decide where to go on her own, without an adult looking over her shoulder. What looks to you like reckless and wildly impulsive behavior may simply be an attempt to let you know that rules need to be adapted to her age and her ability to manage her life. You might want to consider the balance between responsibilities and privileges, and ask yourself, "Would I think this was fair if I were on the other side of this deal?"

When you see what looks like gender, racial, personal, and religious confusion can simply be a part of the process of identifying himself and having that identity validated by the people who matter to him. Again, asking one or two questions and respecting his contributions to any discussion of these issues will allow your teen to formulate his own ideas, clarify his values, and develop his own thinking.

What might feel like hurtful and unreasonable criticism or rejection of your actions and beliefs may simply be your teenager's attempts to explore and clarify his own sense of social justice. Try to remember what it was like to challenge your parents' belief systems. If you insist that your teen accepts what you say without question, then he will be unable to consider and create his own ethics.

GOING TO EXTREMES

It often seems that teenagers do everything to extremes. When they are loyal to a friend, they cannot see that the friend can cause them harm or break their hearts. They refuse to accept that the friend takes advantage or sabotages efforts. When they believe in a cause or think they see an injustice, they can become angry or hostile, and they can find themselves unable to consider others' opinions or viewpoints.

When teenagers seem to be doing whatever they can to get away from their own families, they are not so much running from their siblings, parents, and grandparents as they are running toward people and situations that appear to be far more interesting and exciting. People who laugh at conventional rules and don't want to control everything are very appealing to teens who are pretty sure they are ready for the adult world. When your teenager does things that seem totally out of character and inexplicable, he is not so much impulsive as he is adventurous and yearning for independence.

LIMITS AND STANDARDS

Keeping the context in mind can help when random thoughts and unexpected behaviors pop up. This might help when panic threatens to set in. Teenagers appreciate knowing the limits—as long as they are not the same limits you set when they were ten. They want to be clear about what is expected and where things can give a little. They want you to be willing to listen and consider their point of view. Your teenager doesn't want you to cave on everything and let her have whatever she says she wants because she needs you to be her safety net. She needs to be able to blame you for her reluctance to drink, stay out until all hours, or use drugs. Her strict moral code allows her to hold you to very high standards, and she will be the first to point out those times when you don't live up to your professed beliefs. You are expected to be clear about what you believe, to act accordingly, to defend your beliefs, to hold steady in the storm of your teen's daily-changing perspectives, and to be reasonable and flexible at the same time. This is no easy job!

WHEN THINGS GO WRONG

There is nothing harder than that moment you realize your child is placing herself in danger. Your first reaction might be, "How could I have let this happen?" You might ask yourself what kind of parent you have been, questioning the freedom you granted, wondering about the times you gave yourself a break and didn't ask enough about where she was going or with whom she was going. You might be angry with yourself because you had a sense about the kids she was spending time with.

You might be stunned to recognize that your child is looking and acting like the kind of kid you wouldn't want your child to hang out with. You might wonder if, when you pushed and she pushed back, it caused her to turn away from all the values you hold. You might wonder if you were too strict or too permissive or too busy to notice. You might want to focus your energies on what you could have done, on what other kids have done to influence your children, or on what someone else should have done to protect your child:

- "Why did I let her go out with that boy?"
- "Why did I give in and say she could spend the night with that girl when I knew something wasn't right?"
- "Why hasn't the school expelled that boy? Everyone knew he was selling drugs. It was only a matter of time before he entrapped my daughter."
- "Where did I go wrong?"

The "should haves" give you a little time to breathe when you are faced with a crisis, but they need to be short-lived.

GETTING HELP

When it comes to drugs, alcohol, and behaviors that put your teenager's heart, soul, and life in danger, you will need to buckle up and confront the situation in front of you with courage and determination to protect your child—from dangerous people and dangerous behavior and from himself if necessary. Whether you are faced with a teenager who is drinking to excess, engaging in sexual behavior, using drugs, or injuring himself by cutting or unhealthy eating habits, the only logical response is to face it right back.

This is a battle that must be won now because it will not just clear itself up. Finding a professional who shares your belief in your child and who sees this behavior as a sign that your child is in trouble and not "just being a kid" can be challenging. Referrals from school administrators or a trusted rabbi or pastor can be helpful. The only way to find out if you have located the right person to work with your child is to schedule time to sit down and ask lots of questions about them and what they believe about teenagers.

This is not the time to hand your son or daughter over to someone who claims to have all the answers or who minimizes the danger inherent in these behaviors. Teenagers can benefit from working with a therapist or counselor who acknowledges their struggles, reinforces the values they have been taught, and encourages them to treat themselves and their futures with care.

When your teen goes off course—when she does something that goes against the values and standards you hold—she needs you to respond with a cool head. Give yourself some time and privacy to react the way you want to in the moment before you react the way you should. She needs to know that you will stand by her while you stand by what you have said and what you have taught her.

THE RIGHT QUESTIONS

If you ask your son why he snuck out of the house in the middle of the night or what he was thinking when he skipped school, you will likely get a response that doesn't help the situation at all. Asking, "How could you?" or "What were you thinking?" will likely elicit shrugged shoulders, maybe tears, maybe a wildly fabricated story, or maybe silence and a look that says, "I don't care what happens now." Obviously, this will not help you or your teenager move toward a resolution.

Instead, try asking, "What is happening here?" or "Please tell me about this." Then wait as long as it takes for him to explain. When he does tell you his story, whether you think it's complete or not, whether you think it's true or not, let it play out. In this highly emotional moment—when your teen is scared, maybe angry, maybe even regretful—it is best if you focus on behavior and what comes next. Now what?

Jeannie

Imagine your daughter Jeannie snuck out of the house in the middle of the night. You were waiting for her when she returned. She told you, "Tommy [her boyfriend of two months, a guy you aren't crazy about] and I had a terrible fight after the football game because he thought I was flirting with another guy. When he dropped me off, he was still so mad at me! Then he texted me and said he couldn't sleep until we made up, and I couldn't sleep either, so I went out to meet him."

There are so many red flags here! There are so many things that need to be addressed, and your danger radar is going off like crazy. Take a breath. Repeat clearly what Jennie has done, but limit yourself to her behaviors and the rules she violated. Remember, focus on objective information in this very emotional moment. Put everything else in your pocket to be reviewed and addressed later.

You could say, "Jeannie, you left the house in the middle of the night without permission. Regardless of where you were going or with whom, this was not something we would have given you permission to do. It was dangerous and dishonest of you to leave without permission."

When considering and presenting your child with consequences, you need to be specific and, once again, objective. "You will never see Tommy again" is a mistake. Leave Tommy out of this! Focus on Jeannie. If you are too upset to consider reasonable consequences, say so. Ask Jeannie to consider possible consequences, and tell her you will do the same. Set a specific time—within the next twenty-four hours—to return to this conversation and to determine specific consequences, how they are connected to what Jeannie has done, and how long they will last. Finally, provide a way for Jeannie to make things better. Ask her to think about a way that she can begin to regain her connection with her family, perhaps by helping a younger sibling with homework or by helping with additional chores at home.

When you have arrived at a set of reasonable consequences that will allow you time to consider and address the other concerns you have about Jeannie and Tommy's relationship, talk to Jeannie. Be sure to let Jeannie propose her consequences first; she may surprise you with a much more severe consequence than you were considering. In that case, you can explain that, because this is her first violation, you don't think six months of being grounded is necessary. At the same time, she may be signaling that she needs some time away from Tommy so that he and she can both move on to other relationships. A month's restriction on going out at night will give Jeannie and Tommy some space.

She might also come up with a consequence that has no connection to what she's done. She might suggest that she be required to do all the laundry or that she has to quit the dance team. This is the time to explain that doing the laundry might be a way for her to make amends at home, but quitting the dance team is not something you would consider—because she made a commitment to the team. (You might also wonder if this idea came from Tommy, who wants her to be more available to him after school.)

A new house rule requiring that all cell phones be placed on a charging station in your room every night at 11:00 p.m. will address the middle-of-the-night texts. Explaining that this is an area that you wish you had addressed earlier because it might have protected Jeannie from making the mistake to begin with will allow her to see that you recognize your responsibility to adjust your behavior when what you have been doing has not worked.

Letting Jeannie know that she will need to come home right after school or after dance team practice every day and that she will not be going out at night for one month unless she is with the family or has a school or team commitment will give her specific information to process. This will also allow you to establish a distance between her and Tommy until you can begin to address your concerns in that area.

This is one of those times when Jeannie won't like you very much, and she will likely want to negotiate changes. It is important for you to acknowledge that she is unhappy with your decision and to assure her that you have thought it through very carefully. Give her time to digest your words. A week from now, when the first party comes up, Jeannie will want you to cave in and let her go. She will cry, and she will accuse you of ruining her life, senior year, relationship with Tommy, and so on. Hold on.

Regarding the relationship: Tommy got "really mad" because he thought Jeannie was flirting. Whether she was or not, Tommy and Jeannie have only been dating for two months. Then, he decided that they needed to resolve the situation in the middle of the night, requiring that she violate her family's trust in order to meet his needs. More concerning still is the fact that Jeannie acquiesced.

Jeannie would benefit from seeing a counselor, someone who can help her to see the dangers in this type of relationship, someone who can help her develop the skills she needs to hold her own with others who make demands on her. Jeannie's reaction to Tommy's demands, if left unaddressed, can become a relational pattern for her. Right now, it appears that she can easily be manipulated into accepting someone else's standards for appropriate behavior. A good counselor will help Jeannie to see this for what it is and to consider how this willingness to go along can land her in an abusive or controlling relationship.

Once you have located someone who will address this with Jeannie—preferably a woman—the first appointment should include you and Jeannie. This will give you an opportunity to express your concerns to an objective listener and to Jeannie—concerns about Jeannie's willingness to take blame for "flirting," her acceptance of his getting "really mad," and her agreement to violate her family's rules to assuage his feelings. Your focus on Jeannie's decisions, her good character, and your belief in her ability to manage her future with some support and some good strategies will allow Jeannie to be open to a counselor who can work on those things with her. Your refusal to blame Tommy for your daughter's behavior will allow her to consider his role in the situation without having to protect him from your judgment.

Billy

Imagine your son Billy cut math class and went with two friends to McDonald's. The principal was waiting for them when they returned to school. The principal called you and has advised that he will discuss consequences with his teacher and let you know tomorrow.

Billy tells you, "I don't know why I skipped." And you wait and you wait and you wait. And if you wait long enough, you hear, "I hate math class. It's so boring, and the teacher hates me. He makes fun of me when I get things wrong, and everyone laughs at me. Jimmy had his new car, and he and Joe were going to McDonald's, and I was hungry because lunch sucked today, so I just went. We got back in time for the next class, and if the math teacher didn't hate me so much, he never would have reported me absent because people skip his class all the time, and they never get in trouble for it."

Again, this is way more information than you can deal with in the moment. Focus on Billy's behavior, and save everything else for later. Billy has violated your trust, and he has broken a school rule. The school will have a consequence for his behavior—possibly suspension—and the teacher may have a consequence for his behavior. Ultimately, though, you need to address Billy's decision, and there needs to be a personal consequence connected to the behavior. In this situation, it makes sense to put off your decision until you know exactly what the school and the teacher have planned. You have time for Billy to consider what he thinks might be an appropriate outcome and to think about possible ways he might reestablish a trusting relationship with his family.

If the school administration considers a first-time skip something that parents can deal with rather than something that requires suspension, then that's good for you and for Billy. If not, you will have to live with it and make plans for Billy to do lots of schoolwork on his suspension day—and you will absolutely need to be home with him.

If the teacher lets you know that he will give Billy a zero for missing class, there will be no value in challenging his decision. However, it is important to set a date and time for a conference with the teacher so that you can figure out what's going on with Billy in his class. What consequences can you consider?

Consequences are most effective when they connect with the behavior, but don't pile on too much. Billy needs a way to reconnect with the family values of honesty, commitment, and responsibility. Billy's decision to leave school, regardless of how he feels about the teacher, regardless of how hungry he was, was a violation of trust. He gave in to the temptation presented by Jimmy and Joe and that new car, and that is disappointing because you all have talked about how to say no when faced with peer pressure.

Requiring that Billy come home immediately after school every day for the next month and that he write a letter of apology to his teacher and to school administrators will give Billy time and opportunity to get himself back on track. At the same time, working with Billy to come up with a way that he can repair his relationship with his family by contributing in a special way is important. The message here is more subtle, but Billy's family connection will be strengthened, and that reminds him of what's important.

Maybe he can help his younger sister with her math homework—especially because he is not feeling so great about his own math skills lately. Again, it is unlikely that Billy will be happy about your decisions. You can learn to live with that. You are the grown-up, after all. After some time (but not too much) has passed, it is important for you to revisit Billy's comments about his math teacher and the class.

Should Billy attend the conference with his math teacher, or should you go it alone? This is a decision you will make after talking with Billy. You know your son best. Will it be productive for him to hear what you and the teacher have to say, or is Billy too young, too emotional, or too hurt to participate? Making a list of questions beforehand will allow you to manage your naturally emotional response to the fact that Billy's teacher has been picking on him, or at least that's how Billy feels.

It is not productive to accuse the teacher of humiliating your son, but you will want to find out if that is something that he does with regularity with other students or just with Billy. You will want to find out if the teacher feels his techniques have been effective with Billy in terms of Billy's learning and participation in the class. Maybe the teacher thinks Billy is okay with the teasing.

Ask the teacher if Billy is doing his homework, if he is contributing to the class in a positive way, if he is disrupting the class, or if he is disengaged in class. The answers to these questions, with some specific examples of each, will help you and Billy to address the behaviors effectively. Does the teacher believe the work is too hard for Billy? Is Billy lacking some background skills required for success in the class? You will want to walk away with a clear picture of how the teacher sees Billy and of whether Billy can manage the class—the academic requirements and the dynamics between Billy and the teacher. This information will serve as the foundation for what you do next.

If Billy is disengaged or acting up in class, then he needs to know that is not an effective way to handle his difficulty with the teacher or with math. If the teacher thinks that Billy is being too sensitive or if you can sense that he doesn't like Billy or feels that Billy cannot manage the academic demands of the class, then you will need to meet with an administrator to advocate for change for Billy. If the teacher misread Billy and wants to repair his and Billy's relationship, and if he feels certain that the material is not too hard for

Billy, then all of your efforts need to be focused on encouraging Billy to work with his teacher and to continue in the class.

While no one enjoys these kinds of situations with their teenagers, everyone will go through at least a couple of them as their teens grow up. The good news is that, if you can keep your cool, listen to, and work with the adults involved in the situation and listen carefully to what your kids are saying and not saying, then your chances of a successful outcome improve. If you give yourself time to come up with reasonable consequences and if you address any underlying issues, then you will find that these tough times can ultimately strengthen your relationships with your children and give you a more complete picture of their lives and their perception of themselves.

CONSISTENCY, FLEXIBILITY, PREDICTABILITY

Teenagers are engaged in the hard work of figuring out who they are today and what kind of person they want to be tomorrow, next month, next year, and even twenty years from now, and you will have to hold on for a wild ride. The key is not to let go; the key is to stay with it and stay with them. This is not the time to rework your own teenage years, and it is certainly not the time to panic when things don't go as you think they should. Take some deep breaths, get yourself together, and try to keep things in perspective, ever aware that your teenager needs to see a clear image of what it looks like to be a reasonable grown-up and a loving parent who will stand with him no matter what.

"I HATE YOU!"

It can be so hard to be disliked by your children! Your teenager is still that child you handed your heart to sixteen years ago; it's just that right now she's not being so gentle with your heart. Hard to take after those many years of her thinking you were the best and smartest people in the world! The only reasonable response to this statement is, "I am so sorry that you feel that way right now. I choose to believe that you love me as much as I love you and that what you mean is that you hate that I am imposing these rules [or consequences] on you."

HOUSE RULES FOR EVERYONE

House rules should be reasonable and clear. Every member of the family should be confident that he or she will be treated with respect. Consider the following rules:

- We will not shut one another out.
- We will eat meals together.
- We will come home when asked—both parents and kids.
- We will look at one another when we speak or are spoken to.
- We will not roll our eyes at one another or make fun of one another in a way that hurts.
- We will not swear or scream at one another.
- We will say we are sorry, and we will mean it when we say it.
- We will make amends.
- We will listen to one another when we disagree, understanding that some of us are still children and some of us are still the adults responsible for them.

These are not complicated rules, and there are not thousands of them. They are rules of civility that will allow all members of the family to be heard, to be respected, and to grow.

LETTING THINGS GO

Parents do have to be willing to let some things go and to acknowledge that there are some things they can't budge on. If you are raising a house full of active children, then maybe you can stand sweaty clothes and shoes left everywhere. Maybe most of the time you can tolerate having those active children play ball in the house.

However, maybe you simply cannot tolerate a teenager turning his back on you or rolling his eyes when you're talking to him. Make sure that, when you correct your kids, it's about something important and not just nitpicking at every little thing. Always, always, always make sure your kids understand that disrespect in any form will not get them anywhere. Knowing yourself—what you can tolerate and what you cannot bear—and understanding that your teen needs you to be really steady and mature can help you to create a home that works for you and for your child.

Most teenagers are interesting, principled, funny, and loving. They are also fragile and ever evolving, and they want to know that they are loved, no matter what. They need to know that the adults they love are aware of their challenges and willing to do what it takes to keep them safe and will allow them the freedom to move themselves toward adulthood.

You will be challenged all along the way to be aware and to stay involved, but do not stay too involved. You are expected to allow for more freedom but not so much that your kids fall off the rails. It is a balancing act, and it's not always so much fun. It can be tough to tell a fifteen-year-old that failing math in ninth grade will affect his college options, but it will. A cumulative GPA is affected significantly by a poor showing in ninth grade. It can be disheartening for the star athlete or the aspiring actress to discover that they are no longer the best, even to the point of being cut from teams, orchestras, or casts.

You have now moved from the sidelines to the bleachers. You are a huge fan—trusting her to make reasoned choices and encouraging her to come to grips with disappointments and to decide on next steps. Whether she decides to recommit to more practice, more training, and more effort or chooses another course, this is her process. You can advise and support her, but you can't do it for her. Your teenager is heading straight for adulthood, and you don't want to get in the way.

Chapter 12

Social Life of Teenagers

BEING PREPARED

Before the driver's ed class, before the first homecoming dance, before the first party, you need to consider how you will handle these opportunities for your teen. Both parents need to be on the same page, especially at this time, as teenagers are smart and intuitive about which parent will be more receptive to which request. Recognizing that flexibility and consistency are key, some general principles are helpful.

If you decide that your daughter will not date before she is sixteen but that group activities are fine or that your son will not drive the car at night before he has proven himself to be a mature driver for six months, then you will need to be willing to stick to those decisions together. It is especially important to communicate those decisions to your teen. This way you will avoid the bickering and begging that can become relentless and overwhelming. If you play everything by ear and make decisions in the moment, you will not have time to consider the options or risks inherent in the activity your teen is pursuing, and she will know that, if she keeps at it, she can likely wear you down.

It is important, though, to revisit some of your stricter policies periodically, as teenagers mature quickly and they are meant to be having fun when they are in high school. If you restrict them from most of the fun that other teens are having, they will find a way to circumvent your rules, or they will be unhappy teens.

THE GRASS LOOKS GREENER . . .

Once teenagers get to high school, they encounter all kinds of kids. They realize that not all families operate as theirs does, and some of those radically different family systems look appealing. The kid whose parents let him drink at home or the one whose parents travel a lot and leave him home alone can appear to be lucky.

Faced with natural teenage desires to be free of rules and restrictions, it's important to remember that your teen still wants you to be parents, and he still wants and needs you to protect him—just less and more subtly. You need to be smart, though, and not assume that the parents of your children's friends have the same values that you have. If your child is spending a lot of time at a friend's house, you had better know a few things about the people who run that house. If teenagers consider a mom or dad to be "really nice," or if a mom prides herself on being the "cool mom," then your radar should be up. Are the parents even home? What are their thoughts on supervision of teenagers? Specifically, are they okay with kids drinking, smoking pot, or having sex?

Take the time to reach out to the parents of your children's friends. A private adult conversation about teenagers and adults and the relationships between them can give you a good understanding of the people supervising your teen when you are not around. If you find that your teen's friends' parents have a far different approach to supervision, then you don't need to waste energy trying to convince them that they're wrong in their approach. You just need to understand that that is their approach and that you are tasked with protecting your child from dangerous situations. It will take some creativity to figure out ways to adeptly redirect the friendship and to ensure that your teenager and his friends spend their time after school and in the evenings at your house.

POOR CHOICES

It is likely that your teenager will make choices that you don't understand or agree with. In those moments, your response needs to be measured. You need to ask yourself, "Is my child putting herself in danger?" You need to decide whether to let a poor choice run its course or to step in and stop things. You won't know if you've made the right decision until it's all over with. The ambiguity is almost unbearable, but how will your teenager learn to manage her own life if you don't let her live it while you're still close enough to catch her when she falls?

Strong connection and clear limits are the keys to raising young men and women of self-respect, integrity, and strong character. Keeping connection and encouraging independence—what a challenge! Daughters and sons deserve your support with this balancing act, and the hard work and the fits and stops are worth it when all is said and done.

TAKING NEW RISKS

Teens take more risks than they did when they were younger. Girls generally take their risks quietly, with one or two friends or alone. They tend to be more reluctant to advertise their escapades. Teenage boys, though, lean toward more public risks. They might drive too fast. They might need to show off for their friends by doing dumb things like keg stands and swimming pool stunts—sometimes in strangers' pools late at night. They are almost matched by girls in the regular consumption of alcohol and drug use, but they tend to drink to excess and publicly, while girls often drink in small groups or alone. While teenage boys might be impulsive, as demonstrated by temper flare-ups or sudden decisions to turn left toward Burger King instead of right into the school parking lot in the morning, most of their risk-taking behavior is considered.

Millions of dollars and thousands of hours have been spent teaching teenagers about the risks of dangerous and drunk driving, unprotected sex, and drug use. The incidence of these behaviors has remained steady over the years. It's not that they don't know! Their decision-making process usually goes something like this:

1. The teen is aware that the risk he is about to take doesn't always result in negative outcomes. Not all kids get caught stealing. Not all kids' parents find out they have been drinking, and if they do find out, lots of them don't do much anyway. Not all kids who drive recklessly or even while drunk have accidents.
2. He sees what his peers are doing, and it is very important to him to remain in their tribe.
3. He overestimates his ability to manage the situation. His ego gets in the way of his good judgment. Most importantly, he believes he is invincible and lucky. He and his friends believe that only kids who are unlucky end up permanently injured or dead after drunk driving. They are convinced that only fools lose thousands of dollars on gambling sites. They are certain that will never happen to them. They're too smart, too lucky, and too capable to have that kind of outcome.

Channeled risk taking may at least reduce a teenager's need to take dangerous risks. Involving her in rock climbing, white water rafting, marathon runs, and other significant physical challenges will create the same dopamine high that more dangerous activities produce. Of course, if your teen is involved—sports, extracurriculars, volunteer projects, or a job—she will have far less time and energy for dangerous risk-taking behavior.

FALLING IN LOVE

It is likely that, sometime during their teenage years, your child will fall in love. You may know nothing about this, or you may feel like you know way too much about this first love interest. Teenage love affairs can occur quickly, existing only as a distant crush one day and becoming an all-consuming attraction the next.

The initial stages of a teenage relationship may include no actual conversation or contact at all. It may simply be an idea or a conversation about the other person with friends or an imaginary future romance. If there is some mutual interest, then children will begin flirting. The two young people actually speak, joking and teasing one another or simply commenting on classes or teachers.

If both parties are brave and they move forward with their relationship, then they will put their relationship on display. They might walk to classes together, even holding hands. They can attend events together, excited to make their new relationship public. Posting pictures of themselves as a couple and using *we* whenever they discuss plans can publicize their connection and let others know that they are committed to one another, at least for as long as this love lasts.

When the relationship has held on for a while, maybe a month or two, the teens often become comfortable with one another, much like they might have with a best friend. They can rely on one another and confide in one another. There is likely a strong sexual attraction, and they might do their best to arrange times to be alone. There is a little less excitement during this stage, but within the relationship, sexual attraction can become a significant factor. When one teen wants to engage in more sexual activity than the other, tensions can increase. There is the danger that one party will become frustrated and break off the relationship. There is also a danger that one partner will engage in sexual activity simply to keep the other partner happy or to sustain the relationship. This is the "If you love me, you will do this for me," scenario. The imbalance created in this situation can result in serious consequences and likely an eventual end to the relationship.

If your teen is in a relationship, it is important for you to be aware of how it affects the rest of his life. Is he skipping other activities that were previously important to him? Is he no longer hanging out with friends? Do you have trouble finding out where your teenager is or has been on the weekend? Is he lying to you about who he is with or what he is doing? Are his grades falling? Is he noncommunicative, shut off, or angry when you ask about where he's been or what he's been doing? Is he spending the hours when he's home behind a closed door? Has he cut off communication with his friends?

All these are signs of something that must be addressed. There is a thin line between teenagers being in love and teenagers being obsessed with one another or with the idea of a relationship. If you cannot get through to your teenager, then you need to seek professional help. Find a counselor who can work with your child to examine the impact this relationship is having on the rest of his life.

When, almost inevitably, the teenage love relationship ends, teens can become withdrawn, crying a lot and isolating themselves from the relentless curiosity of their peers. They might also feel a sense of relief because the relationship was limiting their life experiences.

Not unlike many adults, teenagers often hold unrealistic expectations for what their first love can be. Influenced by movies, books, songs, and social media, they expect the drama and excitement to continue forever, and when it doesn't, they are disappointed or confused. They might wonder if there is something wrong with them if they don't have much interest in a love relationship because they don't find it all that fulfilling or because their love interest has broken off the relationship.

This is when you can provide gentle reminders of their incredible worth and the wonderful prospects that lie ahead while combining that with genuine empathy for their current sadness. Judgments, lectures, boyfriend or girl-friend bashing, and suggestions for new love interests are not helpful at this point. Be prepared to listen, empathize, and be present for your teen. Remain aware of the time it takes your teen to recover from sadness, and know the signs of teen depression.

TEENAGE SEXUALITY

If adults understand relationships, commitment, and self-respect, can they simultaneously believe that sex between teenagers is safe? Are parents so fearful of alienating their children that they inadvertently condone and even encourage vulnerable children to give themselves over to someone they will not even like in another six months and even may not remember in five years?

When a teenage girl gives her body to another person, she gives her soul and heart along with it; she can't get anything back completely. There is almost no chance that the recipient of this incredible gift realizes or appreciates what it is that she has done. Is it fair to encourage a teenage boy, still a child at heart, to "sow his wild oats"? Or is he being asked to close his heart off to the fact that he is taking advantage of an innocent friend who likes him? In a society where life is cheapened in every way—through violence, blatant promiscuity, and sexualization of children—don't parents have a responsibility to fight back?

It can be incredibly difficult to discuss sexuality with a teenager for a number of reasons. Embarrassment is a huge factor. There's no telling who might be more embarrassed, the teen or the adult. Built on a foundation of self-respect and respect for others that you have been teaching since your teen was small, a conversation about sexuality can flow naturally.

At this point in her life, your teen has developed her own impressions and opinions about sexuality, sexual activity, and all that might encompass. Ask general questions like, "What are your thoughts about kids having sex before they are adults in a committed relationship?" or, "What do you think teens mean when they say they are in a 'committed relationship'?" Then wait, however long it takes, for the answers.

Watching movies or television shows with your teen can provide lots of opportunities for nonthreatening conversations about sexuality and sexual relationships. Ask him what he thought about the way the characters related to one another or how he would have felt had he been in the relationship on the screen. Make general conversation.

When you approach the subject of sexuality with your teen who is in a relationship, you might start with a simple, "Please talk to me about your relationship with Johnny." It is important to wait and listen. Let her talk. If you can manage to stay quiet and present, she will eventually talk. Try not to panic. You may not want to start with, "Are you having sex with Johnny?" unless you are pretty sure she is. Then, if she feels she's mature enough to have a sexual relationship, you can expect her to be mature enough to discuss that relationship with you—where she sees it going and how she manages the relationship.

Express concern to your son if you feel that the couple is becoming isolated from others: "We don't see many of your other friends these days, and I notice that you seldom go to parties or dances anymore. You and Mary are together so often, and usually it's just the two of you. I know that you are physically attracted to one another, and I am concerned that you might find yourselves in a sexual relationship for which you are unprepared."

Of course, these are awkward situations to address. But if you don't talk about them with your teen, it could well appear that you are afraid of what is happening or that you just don't want to know. If you decide not to know, then you decide to abdicate your parenting responsibilities to two young people who are in the throes of sexual attraction. Their decisions might not be the most reasoned or rational.

If your child is in a sexual relationship, you want to make sure that both teens are protecting themselves from pregnancy and sexually transmitted diseases. You also want to make sure that both are willing participants in sexual activity and for the right reasons. Questions like, "What made you decide that you wanted to have sex with Mary?" or "Can you talk me through how you and Mary made the decision to have sex?" will allow him to examine his choices safely and will allow you to make some determination about your child's maturity level and about the relationship itself.

Remember that even if you think this relationship is destined to fade, this is not the time to criticize the decision or the partner choice. If you have serious concerns about the relationship, however, you will want to consider professional counseling for your child. You are still a parent, and you still have a responsibility to provide your child with guidance, even if it is coming from another source.

Your teen will make leaps and bounds during the six short years before he turns twenty. For at least four of those years, he will be with you but not much. He will want to be with his friends and involved in school activities. He may fall in love and out again more than once. He will seemingly create a new persona every six months or so.

As your teen matures, you will get brief glimpses of the remarkable adult she will one day be, and at the same time, you will see that precious baby that you held in your arms and pushed on the swings just yesterday. Teenagers are interesting, clever, funny, confounding, and changeable. They count on you to hold steady in the storm while adjusting your sails depending on their needs.

Will

Will was an exceptional athlete, destined for a college scholarship for baseball. He was the younger of two children, and his older sister was off in college. His parents were quiet and caring, and both were successful in their careers.

David Keller was the eldest of a big family. He and Will went to school together, and Will was always at the Kellers' house. He loved the chaos and the activity, and everyone in the Keller family loved Will. Will's parents also often enjoyed spending time at the Keller house after the boys finished their high school games.

The two boys often went out with their girlfriends together. They went to parties and dances. The girls were delightful and smart. Everyone seemed to be having a great time in high school. Things changed about midway through their senior year, however. Will's girlfriend was pregnant. Two perfectly wonderful young people with their lives ahead of them; two caring, attentive sets of parents taken by surprise.

Will's parents decided that he would no longer have any contact with the girlfriend. They did not want anything to damage his prospects. He was headed to a good college with a baseball scholarship, and they would not allow this to derail his progress. Will's girlfriend's parents supported her decision to have her baby, and they planned to take care of her and her baby until she could live on her own. When the baby was born, Will managed a secret trip to the hospital to visit his son, but things were forever changed for him and his baby's mother.

Will went on to college, and his former girlfriend went on to being a mother. The following summer, David and a number of his friends came together at the Kellers' house. Will was home from college—with a new girlfriend on his arm. Will's old girlfriend, the mother of his son, came to the party, too. They did not exchange more than a few words.

What this young girl had believed to be true love had simply been a passing thing—at least for Will. He was still a boy—a boy incapable of managing the consequences of his behavior. His parents, in their need to create the future they wanted for Will, did not allow him to fulfill his responsibilities to his child and that child's mother.

Today, Will's son is almost a man himself, soon to graduate from college. His mother never married but instead focused all her energies and efforts on raising her son well and getting an education for herself. She is a successful woman, and she is a good mother.

The man who could have been a father to his son? He is married with young children. He never got to know his first child. They both have missed so much. Now that he has a family, Will might want to talk to his children about relationships, love, respect, avoiding mistakes, and living with the ones they will inevitably make.

Chapter 13

School Life of Teenagers

BALANCING ACT

They often look like adults, but they are not adults, no matter how they look, no matter what they might tell you. They don't reason like adults, so don't be surprised when they do dumb stuff. They still need someone else to be in charge.

It's important to remember that it's not personal—it's just teenage development. As you correct them and let them know how they should act, you will need to maintain an even-handed, almost objective attitude. Think of a traffic cop making a stop along the side of the highway: "Ma'am, I get that you're upset, frustrated, angry, sad, trying to establish your innocence. I, though, still have to do my job. When you drive ninety miles per hour in a fifty-mile-per-hour zone, I have to give you a ticket."

Teenagers are balancing their need to develop relationships with others with preparing for their futures and maintaining ties with their families. They are increasingly aware of what is happening in the world outside their homes and schools, and they are more tuned in to conflicts or struggles within their own family homes. It makes perfect sense, then, that they can become frustrated, anxious, and even angry. School is their job. Whether they are preparing for the world of work or for further education, much of the stress they feel arises from the demands of school.

After you help your freshman register for classes, you will be a peripheral player in your teen's academic life. You will need to stay tuned, checking report cards and going to conferences. Your teen can and should make decisions about the work he will do, the classes he will take, how hard he will work, and what his aspirations for the time after graduation are.

HIGH SCHOOL

It's probably a good thing that most adults do not get the chance to sit in a high school classroom or try to navigate their way through a crowded high school hallway. If adults were able to spend much time in a high school—any high school—they might lose a lot of sleep reconsidering their decision to send their precious, sheltered child to school.

If you are sending your fourteen-year-old daughter to a large coed high school, then she will be navigating those crowded hallways along with eighteen- and nineteen-year-old men. She will need to have her wits about her just to make it from one class to another. In the classroom, she had better be ready to hold her own—asking questions when she needs to and participating in class discussions even if she is painfully shy and nervous.

If your fourteen-year-old son is attending classes with young women who dress provocatively, then it might be very difficult for him to focus his attention and his concentration on schoolwork. He's going to have to figure out a way to adjust because the girls will not change the way they dress so that he can concentrate on Algebra II.

High school teachers will not hold your child's hand or yours. Their expectations for timely submission of assigned work and the standards they hold for good work are not particularly flexible. You will, as a result, find yourself relegated to the position of coach, encourager, and observer at home. You will no longer be expected to advocate (interfere?) for your child with his teachers.

NINTH GRADE

Most high schools do a good job of orienting ninth-graders to the building and the routines before the older students arrive, but nothing can prepare children adequately for the culture shock of high school. If your son attends an all-boys high school, then he will immediately find that there are rituals and practices that come close to the line of hazing but do not usually cross it. He will have to deal with upperclassmen who want their books carried or lunches delivered. Hopefully, your boy soon realizes that these practices are a way of saying, "You're now a part of us," and the teasing and testing will establish a connection between him and his older counterparts.

In all-girls schools, these same practices bring new students into the fold. You can talk about these rituals ahead of time, making it clear that there are limits to what is acceptable but also explaining that the motivation behind them is almost always positive.

In a coed school, both boys and girls will be faced with all kinds of distractions and temptations. Many of these come when freshmen realize that—at least in the beginning—no one even knows they're there. Quieter students may well be overwhelmed by the cacophony that exists in lunchrooms and hallways. Students who have always considered themselves confident leaders may suddenly feel anxious and unsure.

Teens who have gotten used to parents and teachers making sure that they did their homework, studied for their tests, and understood the lessons taught will face the challenges that come with being far more independent with schoolwork. Rarely will a high school teacher check to see if a student has written down her homework or if she has the books she needs as she leaves school.

Rarely will a high school teacher contact a parent about missed assignments until the child has done poorly enough to be failing. Usually about midway through the first quarter, reports will come home that let parents know their son has an F in a class. This is when the panic can set in, and parents realize this is why Johnny says he "loves" school. Johnny is having so much fun in this new world that he has forgotten he's supposed to be studying and doing homework!

Incidents like this provide a good opportunity to review the amount of independence your child has and to discuss with him the measures that need to be in place so that he can bring his grades up before semester's end. It will not do to simply tell Johnny to start studying. Find out what's happening during his day and what's happening on his iPad or iPhone in the evenings. If you restrict use, and set some strict rules for Johnny, you can always loosen them up when you see positive results. Johnny needs to know that you will do what it takes to help him get on track and that, when he gets back to the business of being a student and accepts that he has a responsibility to do his job, you will lessen those restrictions.

TENTH GRADE

Sophomore year is a tough one. The newness has worn off. The academic demands are increasing. Students aren't old enough to enjoy the upper-class privileges, and they are not young enough to be clueless about what they are missing. Teachers do not hold your hands. Those students who are involved in competitive sports or who audition for plays or the band may be told that they aren't good enough for the varsity or the starring roles. Most sophomores can't drive yet, but they are reluctant to ask their parents to drive them to parties or dances, so many of them just opt out of a social life. If your teen wants to ride with an older student to parties or dances, then it is important for you to know this young driver and to talk with his parents about what their thoughts are about him driving a car full of teens around at night. Suddenly it will seem that your child knows lots of young people at school. You might know nothing about them and even might never have seen them. While it's great that your teen is making friends, it is important for you to find out something about these young people before your teen gets in their cars after school.

While the schoolwork itself is more difficult, there is rarely the level of pressure to achieve that's coming. During the tenth grade, students will usually take the PSAT. This is a standardized test that can be used, however carefully and tentatively, to predict success on the SAT. If all goes well, your teen will assume more responsibility for her school obligations, and she will begin to consider her goals for after high school graduation. She will also begin to understand that, if she wants to continue her schooling, then she will need to get good grades so that she will be accepted to college.

ELEVENTH GRADE

Once she survives the doldrums of sophomore year, your teenager will face the high pressure of junior year. SATs and ACTs are taken. She may take advanced placement classes. She may take prep classes for those tests. She may take driving lessons. She will have practice every day after school if she makes the team or the cast or the band. She will have little time left for studying and homework, which are all important now as they will affect college options. Time management and organizational skills will need to be refined and established anew.

The Realistic College Search

When exploring college options, you will need to be straightforward and honest about what you will be able to pay for college and help your children consider options within certain parameters. It might be difficult for you to tell your daughters and sons that certain schools are far too expensive for your budget, but you don't want to set them up for a huge disappointment by letting them apply to schools that are completely out of reach financially.

There is good news, though. Many state-supported junior colleges will guarantee entrance to the state's four-year colleges if students maintain a strong average. Most of those colleges have tuition assistance available. More good news: Most state colleges have excellent programs, and in-state tuitions have remained (relatively speaking) reasonable.

The bad news is that students who attend college can accumulate enormous amounts of debt that will remain with them ten years or more after they have finished school. If you live in New York and your teen wants to go to school in California, then it is important to discuss the limitations on travel that this may cause. Flying home for Thanksgiving, winter holidays, or spring break might be quite expensive and time consuming.

When it comes to applying to schools, it is important to have range of schools as options. This may be the first time your teen faces a significant rejection in his life. It can be hard for a teen to believe that a college might reject him if he has never applied to a school before this. If he has worked hard and gotten good grades, then he may believe that he will get into that elite school. The truth is, however, that he might not get in. Sometimes there is no obvious reason a student gets rejected from a college. This can be very difficult information for a teen and his parents to accept.

College counselors can provide assistance with locating affordable colleges that are good matches for your child's interests, location preferences, grade point average, and financial requirements. These counselors can be very helpful, particularly if you meet with them in junior year.

Preparing for the World of Work

If your teen is planning to enter the world of work after high school, then now is the time to consider the skills she might need to prepare for a career. Are there internships or apprenticeships available to help her prepare? What about local schools where she can receive the training she will need to embark on her new career? Counselors at school should have information available, and it is worth your while to make an appointment for you and your teen to discuss next steps.

TWELFTH GRADE

College applications are due in the fall of senior year. It is the rare parent who is able to get his or her teen to complete the applications in the summer, so the months of October and November can be especially difficult. Once the essays are written and the recommendations are garnered, applications are submitted and the waiting begins. Seniors are often enrolled in rigorous AP classes, but they also have lots of opportunities to choose classes that interest them.

Many high schools offer senior projects, senior internships, or senior privileges that allow students to finish almost all academic work by December. Surely, some of those projects and internships are worthwhile, and just as surely, most seniors are far better served if they are required to remain in their classrooms, working hard until they graduate. The high school years fly by for most families. After having been in elementary and middle school for eleven years, the four short years of high school, with their focus largely on what comes next, seem to disappear in an instant.

The level of competition that exists—between academics and social life—can be intense. Teenagers will often struggle to balance the two. It is worth it to have regular conversations with your teenager about the importance of completing this level of his education and completing it well.

JOB WELL DONE

While you have likely been relegated to the supporting cast as your teen has progressed through these four years, you still have an opportunity to reinforce your values and all those lessons you've taught over the years. Your teen, as she matures, is far more likely to engage in conversation with you. Talk with your teen about the state of the world and current events. Find out her take on controversial subjects. When teenagers speak the unvarnished truth about the way they see the world, it can have a profound effect on the adults who raise them.

One of the best things a parent can discover is that she has a son who wants to contribute in a meaningful way to society by entering a service profession or serving in government or the military. Another one of the best things a parent can discover is that his thoughtful, bright daughter cares deeply about people and wants to spend time volunteering with people who are suffering.

Chapter 14

When Families Break

When families experience divorce, children suffer. There is no doubt about that. Children whose parents decide to divorce need and deserve to have comfort, reassurance, and guidance as they deal with the loss of their family.

Children should not have to choose. It is unfair and unkind to make them choose. Two adults who clearly chose wrong at some point themselves should not put their children in a position of having to choose between them. Divorce is unpleasant, and emotions are intense. What looked like love can turn into a poisonous vitriol, and it can hurt children.

When parents bicker and complain about one another as they negotiate the new reality of joint custody, visitation, and alternate weekends, they only hurt their children. When mothers rant on and on because the children don't get enough sleep at their father's house or fathers complain that the kids don't remember to bring home their school uniforms because their mother is so disorganized, they put their children in an untenable position. The children either have to defend their dad or mom, or they discover that it's safer to blame their parent for everything that goes wrong.

Parents who abdicate their responsibilities by handing their children off to new spouses, boyfriends, or girlfriends and decide to avoid conflicts with exes by just letting them have the kids are only punishing their children. Children need both parents—parents who are mature enough to coexist peacefully and to keep their criticisms of one another to themselves.

For some children, there might be a sense of relief when parents announce their plans to separate or divorce. Tension and discord in the family make children anxious. They worry about what will happen each day and in the future. They wonder if they are the cause of their parents' unhappiness, and they may feel responsible for the sadness and anger they see in their parents.

THE IMPACT OF TENSIONS AT HOME

Fearing that they may be forgotten as the tension mounts, children might begin to act out at school and home as a way of demanding that someone notice them. Others may shut down, so concerned about upsetting things more that they try to disappear. The stress of living in a preseparation/pre-divorce home can become almost unbearable. Children worry that, if they acknowledge the tremendous discord in their home or speak out loud about the possibility of divorce, then they will cause it to happen. So when there is finally a resolution or a plan to deal with the situation, children are relieved to know that someone is taking charge of things. While there is relief, there is inevitably enormous sadness as children witness the end of their family life.

MORE INFORMATION

Oftentimes after the initial announcement, parents become so absorbed in their own grief and the process itself that they ignore their children's need for information about what comes next. It can be difficult to talk with children about emotionally charged situations like divorce, and you may avoid the topic in an attempt to keep from feeling even more guilty and sad. When that happens, children are left feeling that they can no longer rely on their mom or dad to answer their questions and tell them what's happening. They are left feeling isolated and unmoored. Children cannot be expected to manage very strong emotions on their own. They are not equipped to do that.

EXPRESSING THEIR FEELINGS

Children who are in the middle of a divorce will need to be able to say that they don't like their new situation. They also need to know without a doubt that there is nothing they can do to reverse it. It is not fair to let kids think that, if they are good enough or naughty enough or sick enough or needy enough, they can bring their family back together. This needs to be clear to them from the start. If boys and girls think that there is a chance, then they cannot resist trying to convince their parents to return their family to the way it was.

REASSURANCE, PREDICTABILITY, BOUNDARIES

Children need to be reassured that they have one dad and one mom and those people will be their parents forever, no matter who else enters the picture. At the same time, they need permission to love, respect, and appreciate stepfathers and stepmothers.

Predictability—of schedule, routines, expectations, and the people involved in children's lives—can do a lot to ease the stress of divorce for children. If children can experience a consistent schedule of visitations and activities, then they can generally find comfort in knowing at least where and with whom they will be on a given day. The more the boundaries of the parent-child relationship are blurred, the more anxious children can become.

If Mom uses her son as a shoulder to cry on or Dad involves his daughter in trying to collect information on what her mother is doing and when she's doing it, then children are being asked to act as adults, and they will become increasingly anxious and angry. If parental guilt drives dramatic changes in behavioral expectations, then children will become confused and fearful, wondering who is in charge.

An absent, unseen parent is still a child's biological parent, and that child should be allowed to wonder what it might be like to have him or her in his life. There is no way to break the connection between child and parent, and it is cruel to try to do that. As children grow up, they realize that their parents are not perfect, both the ones they have right in front of them and the ones who have gone away. As they recognize the infallibility of all humans, and especially of their own parents, children can also understand that every person is lovable and that perfection is not a prerequisite for loving or being loved.

MANAGING THE FALLOUT

Fears of abandonment are unavoidable when children become embroiled in the business of divorce. Young children may want to sleep with their parents, and their behavior may regress. They may not want to go to school or to the other parent's home—afraid that they will no longer see their mom or dad. The disruptions that accompany divorce can make children feel like they have to hang on for dear life. Moving to a new house, going from one house to another, new routines, and new people can all lead children to be afraid.

When children are allowed to remain in their school with teachers and classmates who know them, they are far more able to separate themselves from the chaos and sadness created by divorce. During their school days, things remain predictable, and this is a true comfort to children.

While every child will react differently to a separation and divorce in the family, there are some commonalities of which you should be aware. Girls often appear to deal with their unhappiness about their parents' divorce by separating it from their day-to-day lives, almost considering it something that happened to their parents, not to them.

If Dad moves out and Mom has primary physical custody, then boys will often experience the effects of being "fatherless" in far different ways and for much longer. Young boys often become noisier, angrier, more restless. They can become disruptive or uncooperative at home and school—almost scream-ing out, "I need someone to notice that I am suffering!"

Adolescents often do their best to distance themselves from what they see as their damaged family. They feel frustrated and embarrassed that their family's shortcomings are now evident for the world to see. Worries about money can lead them to become concerned about their own futures, wonder-ing whether they will have to change schools and lose their friends or whether they will be able to go to college.[1]

FEELING CONFLICTED

Children in the midst of divorce can feel conflicted, unsure about where their loyalties should lie. They often feel betrayed and foolish if they did not see the divorce coming. Teenage brains are not ready to understand the nuances of relationships, and their sense of justice might require that they label one parent as the bad guy or one parent as guilty of causing the other to leave. So while they are angry at the parent who leaves the family, they are often equally angry at the parent who's been left behind for being weak and inadequate.

Children of divorce often feel compelled to take sides and lay blame. If they see their mother as a victim, then boys might challenge her authority, becoming disrespectful and disobedient. Teenage daughters may wonder why their mother wasn't a good enough wife to keep her husband, and teenage sons might wonder if they will now be faced with additional responsibilities as the man of the house. They might even try ordering their mother and sib-lings around in an attempt to ensure stability at home.

Young girls often try to become more adultlike. They might get upset at other children who don't follow the rules in school, needing to know that, at least in school, there is some control and consistency. Both boys and girls will cry more often, whether they do it in front of their parents and teachers or behind closed doors.[2]

Both boys and girls worry. They worry about whether they might lose the custodial parent. They worry that they will have to move, that they will not have enough money to live on, that others will find out about the divorce, and more. If Dad has moved out, then his children likely will miss him intensely, and they can feel that they have been rejected.

When children are distraught and feel powerless, they often experience physical symptoms. Complaints about stomachaches, headaches, and generalized aches and pains can send them to the school nurse. The wide array of emotions and reactions to divorce can be incredibly difficult for young people to manage. Counselors who can work through these emotions with children and their parents are a valuable resource.

It is incumbent on divorcing parents to acknowledge their children's feelings and worries and at the same time reassure their children that they will still parent them. By making sure that everyone has a schedule and advance notice when arrangements change, you can restore some sense of stability in their lives.

TRASH TALK

Children can only make a healthy transition to their new lives if their parents abandon the need to denigrate one another. When adults use their children as weapons in custody battles, no one wins, especially not the children. If you use your children as sounding boards or messengers, then you are essentially asking them to serve as partners or therapists, neither of which they are equipped to do.

Divorce and dissolution of the family is created by adults and affects children. You are responsible to remain available and continue being a parent to your children. When you are faced with your children's tears, shock, anger, and rejection, it's tough. It makes the process of recovery and rebuilding a life for your family difficult. You have no choice but to hold up.

It can be tempting to align yourself with your children's views—accepting the role of victim in order to get a little more sympathy or berating your former spouse to ensure that your kids see you in a positive light. Don't do it! In the end, these choices will only serve to prolong the agony for your children.

Instead, children who experience divorce need constant reminders of their parents' commitment to being parents. They need the regularity of trips to the park and Friday night movies with popcorn. Just because a parent has moved on—to a new social life, new friends, new interests—it doesn't mean that her children are now over it. Children never fully recover from the unraveling of their family, but there are things you can do to help them accept and move on.

NEW PEOPLE IN CHILDREN'S LIVES

Caution is the keyword when inserting new people into children's lives. Your kids have gone through the destruction of their family life as they knew it, and they do not deserve to experience additional losses. Leading children to believe that the next lady or man might be their new parent can cause children to experience the pains of loss all over again when things don't work out. Introducing new boyfriends or girlfriends to your children before you even know that a relationship will last for a month is a recipe for heartache. Because a parent is lonely, she might enter a new relationship, unwisely allowing someone new to move into the home.

After divorce, parents might expect their children to accept and maybe even be grateful for new relationships with caregivers, parents' friends, and love interests. No matter their age, children need to be allowed time to become comfortable with the new people in their lives, and they need to understand clearly what their relationships with those people entail. Little girls and boys should not be expected to express physical affection for their parents' new love interests, but they should be expected to be respectful as they would be with any new adult acquaintance.

Expecting your children to welcome and depend on someone they hardly know is unfair and unwise. Before a child has even had time to get used to the idea that his parents are divorced, he is being asked to welcome a new person into his home, a person who will likely be gone before he knows it. This practice, which is ever more common, encourages children to make an emotional connection that will, in most cases, end abruptly and leave a child feeling rejected, unworthy, and sad.

How many changes can a child endure before he or she falls apart? When a new partner—but not a new parent—begins to act as a parent, disciplining children or becoming physically affectionate, children become confused about boundaries. They will often begin to worry about their own safety, and rightfully so. It is far better to take some time and use good sense to find out if this new love interest is leading to a sustainable relationship. It is just as important, though, to consider that any time and energy you take to date or establish new romantic relationships is time you are taking away from your children, right when they need you to be there the most.

DEALING WITH FEELINGS OF LOSS AND SADNESS

It's important to know that, when you ask your children how they are feeling about the situation, they might not be able to express their feelings in words.

They can't consider their feelings objectively, and they worry that they and you may become overwhelmed by strong feelings. The trouble is, they have to do something with their sadness and confusion.

If they act out at school or at either home, their behaviors can elicit exactly the wrong responses. The scoldings they receive and the frustration they see in their parents and teachers when they act out can isolate them even more from the very people who might be able to help them cope with their situation. At the same time, your children need to know that you will continue to expect them to do the right thing.

They need quiet, comforting recognition of their very difficult feelings, and they need to know that acting out in a negative way will not relieve those feelings. They need to know that getting on everyone's last nerve and pushing everyone away are just the opposite of what they need. They need to know that you will be right there with them, loving them even when they are acting in the most unlovable way.

This is when you really have to take a minute and see your child's behavior for what it is. It's a cry for your reassurance, attention, help, and love. This is when you really must put your own intense emotions and needs aside and understand that your primary responsibility, no matter how difficult it might be, is to help your children mourn a terrible loss and begin to heal.

Think long and hard before bringing a new person into their lives. Provide consistency and as much stability as possible, and make your children a priority as you help them to cope with a true crisis in their lives. If ever you can manage to be the grown-up by focusing on your children's needs, this is the time.

Chapter 15

Skills, Stress, Anxiety, Depression

EXECUTIVE FUNCTIONING SKILLS

What skills do your children need in order for them to be successful in school and beyond? Executive functioning skills will help your child to meet the considerable demands that begin in elementary school and extend to college and beyond.[1] It can be difficult for a child to access executive functioning skills if he is anxious or depressed. As your child approaches middle school and again in high school, you will want to take an inventory. Together, you can identify where he is strong, and where he needs some work.

Impulse and Emotional Control

Children begin to work on these at a very young age. As they discover that it pays to consider things before acting on every desire and feeling they have, they learn to get along with others. While it is not unusual for a kindergarten student to cry and even lash out when she is frustrated, as she gets older she must learn to recognize and manage her emotions in order to function in a school setting.

Working Memory

Children need to keep some information accessible in order to function in school. They study and use such strategies as mnemonics to remember information because they need to access it as they incorporate new information or when they are assessed for learning. If a child is very anxious about something or if the child's home situation is chaotic, then working memory is affected.

Take, for example, the third-grader who studies well for her spelling test. The morning of the test, she cannot find her lunchbox. Her siblings are ready to go to school. Her mother is upset with her because she was supposed to put the lunchbox in the kitchen yesterday when she got home from school. She begins to cry because she does not want to be late for school and she doesn't want to carry her lunch in a brown bag. By the time she gets to school and rushes into her classroom, the other students are just about to begin the spelling test. She cannot access her working memory because she is still processing the upset of the morning.

Task Initiation

Students need to be able to begin new tasks. This can be difficult if a child is anxious, concerned about making mistakes, or distracted or if the child relies so heavily on others for direction and ideas that he cannot bring himself to risk starting a task without someone leading him through it.

Flexible Thinking

Some children (and adults!) have difficulty considering other perspectives or ideas once they have decided that they know what is right. This can create a roadblock to learning. Periodic intentional changes in routine or schedules can help children establish a practice of flexible thinking as they realize that things can be adjusted without catastrophe striking.

Self-Awareness

This is a skill that people work on throughout their lifetimes. Awareness of one's strengths and weaknesses and recognition of one's needs are increasingly necessary as academic and social demands increase. Social awareness is key during the teenage years. Teens need to develop a self-image that is congruent with their values and behaviors.

Planning and Prioritizing

Another lifelong skill is the ability to create plans for accomplishing tasks. Deciding which tasks deserve attention and which ones can wait is a challenge for young people who are inundated with information, multiple demands on their time, and constant contact from the outside world. Allowing even the youngest children to prioritize and plan activities will teach them the importance of these skills.

Stress Tolerance

Stress tolerance is a skill learned experientially. Some stress allows students to get to it and avoid procrastinating. When circumstances change or when life becomes chaotic, stress increases. If a young person understands when to seek help and if he has experience with stress-reduction techniques (exercise, deep breathing), then his stress tolerance will be adequate as demands on his time and energy increase.

No one has all these skills mastered, not even most adults. Depending on life circumstances, some of these will be far more important than others, and some might momentarily abandon your child. Impulse control and emotional control are foundational for students but can disappear temporarily when they are faced with crises, like a death or serious illness in the family, or other highly stressful situations, like the transition to middle school or high school.

It is important for you to do what you can to prepare your child for major transitions and to help him manage his life during those times. When the transition feels overwhelming, he might lose track of things, forget assignments and chores, and become emotional and irritable. He may become convinced that he cannot manage the situation.

Sometimes the simplest things can help. Think about getting an extra set of books to keep at home for your middle schooler or your ninth-grader. Most teachers will have an extra set on hand that you can borrow. This can avert the panic and upset that comes with leaving a needed book at school. Spend ten minutes on Friday afternoon helping your child empty and organize her backpack and binder. She can throw out unneeded papers (and candy wrappers); put important papers in her binder; and make sure she has pens, pencils, and other supplies for the week to come.

Stress results from daily events, like a test or a missed bus, or from chronic situations, like family discord, poverty, and illness. Think of anxiety as an overabundance of stress. It can arise from extended periods of stress or from the intensity of a situation.

ANXIETY

Anxiety is characterized by feelings of dread and fearfulness. The source of the anxiety is not always recognized or reasonable. A child who experiences day-to-day stresses can usually learn to manage and keep them in perspective, and stress can even help him stay on task and maintain a certain energy level. However, anxiety can escalate dramatically when stress is produced by either new and unexpected demands, chronic threats, physical and physiological changes, lack of support, or any combination of these.

WHEN FACED WITH LOSS

When children are faced with the loss or illness of a loved one or a crisis that causes instability in the family, they will experience considerable stress. A parent's job loss, an impending divorce, financial difficulties, or a move to a new home can cause a young person to worry about the immediate and distant future.

Ruminating and worrying about what might happen can cause sleeplessness, irritability, loss of appetite, and an inability to focus—all skills necessary for him to do the work that is expected of him. Without support and the use of some accessible coping strategies, he is more prone to developing high levels of anxiety.

It is important to remember that adults express their grief in very personal ways, and children will do the same. Young children, who still make good use of magical thinking, may come to believe that they have caused someone to die or that they can bring the person back. Telling a child, "We've lost your grandmother," means exactly that to the child. She will wonder when you will find her grandmother. Describing death as a "long sleep" is dangerous, as you could very well end up with a child who is afraid to go to sleep or one who panics when she sees that her grandmother has been put in a box in the ground. She cannot help but wonder what will happen when her grandmother awakes!

Explain that a person no longer needs to breathe or eat when he dies and describe death as irreversible to help your child put aside any worries about the loved one being buried or cremated. It is important to answer your child's questions about the death, and that won't always be easy as you grieve. Be sure that you share the details of the funeral, wake, or other services with your child, and be sure to include him if he wants to be a part of the planning or if he wants to participate in the ceremony itself. By including him in the plans, you will lessen his anxiety and increase his sense of control.

Older children and teens may seem incredibly self-centered as they deal with the news that a loved one has died. They may wonder how this will affect their regular life, such as plans to attend a party or participate in a school event. This is a normal reaction for young people who are naturally self-centered. Even as she advocates for permission to get back to regular life, your teenager will feel some sense of guilt for not being more upset. You can ease that guilt by recognizing and acknowledging that her life should not stop because someone has died, but she is expected to attend the funeral and any other events surrounding the burial.

As time passes and the family adjusts to the loss, it will not be surprising for your child or teen to express sadness about a loved one not being around for special events. He might worry that he will forget what the person looked or sounded like. Creating a photo album for him and talking about the things he cherished about his loved one will help him to experience his grief and then to refocus on his life.

Children and teens who have lost a parent often worry that they will lose their surviving parent. They might become protective of the surviving parent, refusing to acknowledge their own sadness for fear that their mom or dad will fall apart. Rather than asking your teen how he's feeling, you might try acknowledging that a day has been particularly hard for you and wonder if it's been the same for him: "I missed your dad a lot today as I was cleaning out the garden. He always loved getting ready for spring. It was his favorite season. I was remembering how you two would load up the truck with mulch and then spend hours spreading it."

In an effort to protect their children and themselves from the sadness that they feel, many people feel it's best to avoid talking about the deceased loved one altogether. Just the opposite is true. When you bring up positive memories or identify favorite things or moments that remind you of the person, you reaffirm their importance in your lives. Children need to be able to talk about the way they experienced the loss—the news that the person had died, the funeral, and the days after the loved one's death. They need to be able to tell stories about the person they miss without worrying that they will upset others.

Charles

Charles enrolled in a master's course to get a degree in school counseling. The professor discussed the many ways in which teens handle grief and the additional stresses it can create. The professor wondered if any of her students, all of whom were high school teachers, had had a student who lost a parent during the school year. Charles raised his hand and told his story:

> I was an only child. I attended an all-boys high school. I was quiet, but I wasn't a particularly shy kid, and I had a nice group of friends. I played rugby, and I had an active social life until the fall of my junior year. My mom got really sick then, so I started to decline invitations to parties and stuff. I kept going to school, and I acted like nothing was going on while I was there. No one asked me anything. I kept up with my grades because I knew my mom would be upset if I didn't.
>
> Over the Christmas break, my mom died. My dad was completely wrecked. He didn't think to tell the people at my school that my mom had died. When I went back to school after Christmas break, my friends were talking about trips they had taken, stuff like that. I didn't tell anyone my mom had died. What was I going to say: "Oh, yeah, well over my Christmas break, I buried my mother"? I had never felt so lonely.

I guess eventually someone told the people at school because the counselor called me in and wanted to know if I wanted to talk. I didn't. I was angry. I thought they should have known somehow. I had trouble focusing on my work, and I isolated myself from friends who had no idea why I was so closed off. It took me a really long time to get back on track after that.

Charles's unvarnished recounting of his mother's death and the subsequent effect it had on him was painful to hear and illustrated clearly the impact a loss can have on a young person.

LIFE WITH NO BREAKS

The ability to put stress in the proper perspective and to avoid spiraling into anxiety is particularly important for young people today. Children are constantly bombarded with stimuli. They have very little time to catch their breath, recover, and regroup before the next onslaught. It used to be that once children got home from school they could decompress, mentally process the happenings of the school day, and then escape into an activity that gave them pleasure. They could watch television sitcoms or read a book. They could play pickup basketball or ride a bike, all without having to talk with anyone. Today adolescents, teenagers, and sadly some younger children cannot decompress.

The constant intrusion of text messages or updates on Instagram and TikTok, the Netflix binges, Starbucks before and after school, poor diet, and maneuvering through the hallways of school can easily send a young person's system into overdrive and out of balance. When the stressors exceed his capabilities, your child may begin to experience unhealthy stress—the stepping stone to anxiety.

LEFTOVER PANDEMIC ANXIETY

Chronic stress escalated during the pandemic as adults became afraid. Society as a whole experienced an overriding sense of anxiety that often resulted in aggression, hostility, and frustration. The realization that something totally unexpected could turn their lives and the lives of their children inside out and upside down took the most even-tempered and reasonable adults by surprise.

Increased parental anxiety results in increased anxiety in their children. Inadvertently, parents added fuel to the fire, spending time and energy examining all available information, trying to get a grip on what was happening, and what could happen in the future. Even the most attentive parents could not protect their children from the uncertainty and loss of control that intruded on their lives.

For many children, the anxiety has not waned. The parents of young people who are experiencing acute anxiety are painfully aware that the detritus of the pandemic remains. Society is just beginning to grasp the lingering effects of this crisis. The stressors of the pandemic and the massive changes that are occurring in young people's bodies and brains combine to create what is, for some, unbearable stress. They will do almost anything to escape their anxiety. They will avoid whatever scares them, and sadly, almost everything can scare them.

SIGNS AND SYMPTOMS OF ANXIETY

A desperately anxious young person may isolate herself; disengage from parents and friends; or refuse to go to school, eat, or bathe. She may stop talking altogether. Anxiety left unchecked will likely result in a child who experiences signs and symptoms of depression. She may consider suicide as her only escape.

Anxiety is not a character flaw; it exists on a spectrum, and it comes and goes. Children who are anxious are always on the lookout for danger. It takes courage to function with anxiety. Eighty-five percent of teens who are diagnosed with anxiety and depression were first diagnosed with an anxiety disorder. The number 1 misdiagnosis of anxiety is ADHD.[2]

Girls report experiencing anxiety more than boys do. The surgeon general reports that emergency room visits for suicide attempts for adolescent girls in 2021 rose 50 percent from 2019. Suicide was the second-leading cause of death for children ages ten to fourteen and third-leading cause of death for young people ages fifteen to twenty-four in 2020.[3]

Children who are experiencing high levels of anxiety display an array of behaviors in combination. These behaviors are often evident in the school setting and may not become known to parents until after a child has been experiencing them for a while:

- The young person's attention is in and out.
- Intense anxiety is triggered by simple things like a pop quiz.
- He makes frequent visits to the nurse at school.
- She has difficulty starting a task, participating in class discussions, and recognizing when she has finished a task.
- He is sleepy and fatigued during the day: sleepy because he often has trouble sleeping at night and fatigued because he is working hard to keep it together.

- She worries excessively about assignments and grades.
- He taps, hums, and mumbles.
- She is jumpy and overreacts to touch or innocuous comments by others.
- He might hide in bathrooms or locker rooms to avoid large crowds.
- She might refuse to work.
- He engages in ritual behaviors: counting steps, checking light switches repeatedly, straightening desk corners, handwashing, and aligning and realigning paper corners.
- She has particular difficulty returning to school after long weekends or vacations.
- He frequently asks, "What if . . . "
- She appears wary and vigilant.
- He expresses helplessness.
- She cries and expresses fury.
- He appears defiant; has a flat affect; or is excessively emotional, laughing too loudly or speaking over others.
- She appears to be a perfectionist, unwilling to accept that she has completed an assignment and working slowly to be sure everything is right.
- He has difficulty with eye contact.
- She argues excessively.
- He avoids stressful situations, which actually increases his anxiety level.

Anxious children describe their thoughts and feelings in a variety of ways. They say that living with anxiety is like being followed by a voice that uses all your insecurities to threaten you. They describe a knot in the stomach, an inability to take a full breath, and looking and acting normal only as long as no one talks to them. Some teens describe their anxiety as stupid and irrational, and they hate it, but they admit that they can't figure out how to live any other way.

Curtis

Curtis excelled academically in elementary school. He was always awkward, though. He acted younger than his peers and couldn't quite figure out the social expectations they held. It often seemed to Curtis that all the other kids knew the rules, but he had somehow missed learning them. He had friends, but they came and went. He never had a best friend, and he appeared to be okay with that.

When he got to middle school, Curtis was bombarded with all kinds of new expectations and behaviors. He was bright and well prepared academically, so he was able to pass his classes. He was not able to focus in class, though, because he worried that someone would talk to him and he wouldn't know what to say. He was afraid to raise his hand for fear that he would answer incorrectly and the other kids would laugh at him.

They sometimes teased him, and they did laugh at him. He wasn't quite sure what he did to bring on the laughter, but he knew he didn't like it. He started spending lunchtime in the bathroom. He went to the nurse complaining of stomach pains and asking to go home. After multiple visits to the doctor and lots of tests, Curtis's mom took him to a therapist. He was diagnosed with generalized anxiety disorder. The diagnosis didn't mean much to Curtis. He already knew he was anxious.

After a few sessions, he refused to go to therapy. He convinced his mother that it didn't help and maybe even made him more miserable. She acquiesced. Curtis's mom decided that he needed an activity that would help him feel more capable and wouldn't require him to function on a team, so she signed him up for karate lessons. Curtis liked karate until he didn't. He started to feel like people were watching him and laughing at him. Soon, he refused to return to karate classes.

Curtis missed a few days of school each month. Each time he told his mom he "just couldn't go." He became depressed. He lost his appetite. He was tired all the time. When he went to school, he couldn't concentrate, and his grades began to suffer.

His friends avoided him, or at least he thought they were avoiding him. He felt hopeless. Curtis refused to go to school more and more often. He cried and begged his mom not to make him go. Sometimes he told her he wanted to die. He could tell she was scared to push him too hard.

During the summer after eighth grade, Curtis started smoking pot and felt some temporary peace. He lay on the couch or sat in a chair with the television on most of the day. He never went outside. When his mom came home from work, he'd tell her he'd been hanging out with friends at the pool. She suspected that Curtis was lying, but she feared his reaction if she confronted him.

In the fall, Curtis used alcohol and pot to get him through the almost unbearable early days of ninth grade. He stopped going to school in October. His mother threatened to take him to the hospital. He cried. He argued that he'd be able to go back after Christmas break. He begged his mom to leave him be. She saw she was losing what was left of her son. She acted.

Curtis spent several months in the hospital. There he learned to manage his anxiety, and his depression lessened. Curtis and his mom came to accept that his anxiety would never go away completely, but they learned a lot about how to manage it and keep it from overwhelming him. The course of Curtis's untreated anxiety was not all that unusual. His anxiety led him down a treacherous road—right to depression.

WHAT CAN YOU DO?

- Anxious children need help coping and managing their worry.
- Explain what anxiety is and that it exists to protect us in dangerous situations.
- Explain that excessive anxiety is a result of the brain reacting to false alarms, which happens to everyone at some point.
- Do not help your child avoid the things that cause her anxiety. You will only reinforce the idea that something is scary. If you manage every situation that makes your child anxious, you will reinforce for her the idea that she cannot manage her anxiety.
- Don't always speak for your reluctant child.
- Don't answer "what if" questions more than once.
- Work with your child to label what has happened to increase his anxiety: "It will be difficult to go to a new school where they do things differently from what you're used to."
- Reassure him that, while he will still feel anxious, you and he can create a support system that will help him cope: "I know you will feel anxious initially, but eventually, using the printout we put on your binder, you will adjust to the new schedule, and you will know where your classrooms are. At home, we will still have all the same routines. We will still eat dinner together, and you can still do your homework right here so that I can be nearby if you need help."
- Reassure your child that she can gain some control over her thoughts, feelings, and behaviors that result from them. She can learn not to react or respond to every passing thought that she has. She can learn how to breathe through anxious thoughts, to think things all the way through before reacting, and to choose a plan to cope.
- Encourage your child to face his fears, taking small steps and praising him for any attempt he makes toward that end.
- Reinforce her ability to make choices even though she is afraid she will make a mistake.
- Don't control his environment and his decisions. If you assume all control over your child's life, then he will shut down even further.
- If you provide her with constant reassurance that everything will be all right, then she will stop listening.
- If you threaten or panic, you will exacerbate the situation.
- If you resolve to remain steady and present and you learn all you can about anxiety, you can help your child cope.

Perspectives and Game Plans

When your child expresses worry about what might happen in the future—at the birthday party, when she starts fifth grade, if she goes to the pool and her friends aren't there yet—help her gain a present perspective. Ask her to imagine the worst things that could happen in those circumstances, and then maybe even expand those imaginings to the ridiculous. This will allow her to realistically view her anticipated disasters and find a way to laugh at the what-ifs.

If she has legitimate concerns that can be dealt with concretely, then help her to address them. What will she do if her friends have to leave the pool early and she's there alone? Help her explore possible actions to take. She could get out her book and read. She could talk to some other kids. She could swim laps. Notice, you will not suggest that she text you to come rescue her from her discomfort. Instead, you will allow her to find a way to ease her anxiety on her own. Helping your daughter to consider ahead of time the options for action that *she* can take in different situations will hand the locus of control back to her and decrease the stress she is experiencing.

Simple Steps to Lessen Anxiety

You and your anxious child can practice some easy techniques that will help ease the discomforting symptoms that accompany anxiety. Slow breathing, progressive muscle relaxation, identifying and challenging anxious and negative thoughts, journaling, praying a favorite prayer, visualizing positive outcomes, and listening to music can all help to ease anxiety symptoms. These simple strategies can help your child control her anxiety:

- Sitting on or blowing into his hands can keep him from wringing them or keep them from shaking.
- Creating a fist and relaxing it ten times in a row can be helpful.
- Forcing himself to focus on five things can help settle anxiety. This can be something you can do together when he is feeling anxious. Each of you can focus on and identify the first thing you see, the first thing you hear, the first thing you can touch or feel with your fingers or any other part of your body, the first thing you smell, and the first thing you taste.
- Eating a healthy diet, getting enough sleep, and exercising will increase your child's ability to cope with anxiety.
- Getting involved in activities at school or joining a service project will help him focus his energies on others.[4]

Excessive focus on the future and little attention to the present can cause him to miss the beauty of the life that is right in front of him.

CHANGING DYNAMICS IN MIDDLE
AND HIGH SCHOOL

Inevitably, when children enter middle school and again in high school, they will experience shifts in their friendships. If your child chooses to move away from a friend or a group of friends, she may feel guilty, and she may face repercussions from her former friends. Encourage her to write in her journal and talk with you about why she chose to move away from certain friendships. In this way she can confirm that she has made the correct choice and move on.

If the friendship shift was not her choice, then she might experience feelings of shame. Ask her to take some time to look around at school and notice other students who might be people she would like to know. Help her explore ways she might extend herself toward becoming friendly with those students. Joining just one club or getting involved in just one after-school activity will give her the opportunity to slowly and naturally get to know other students. In either case, her anxiety level will increase as she attempts to manage these unfamiliar circumstances. She may need to rehearse at home in order to lessen anxiety at school.

WHEN ANXIETY KEEPS YOUR CHILD
FROM ENGAGING IN LIFE

If anxiety is keeping your child from engaging in normal activities, playing on a team, going to school regularly and on time, playing with friends, engaging with family members, smiling and laughing, and talking and listening, then you need to seek professional help. If he is not sleeping or eating, then you need to seek professional help. If your child has been exposed to a traumatic experience of any kind or if the anxiety seems to be getting worse despite your best efforts to help him cope, then you need to seek help. The chances are very slim that you and your teen will be able to manage his anxiety if it's so debilitating that it keeps him from engaging in his own life. Fear of being judged, fear of a diagnosis, or fear of the treatment to come cannot be allowed to keep you from taking action.

THE ANXIETY-DEPRESSION CONNECTION

Chronic or intense anxiety can lead to depression in young people, in particular children who are experiencing the significant changes that accompany the transition from child to adult. The signs and symptoms of depression in children and teens are varied. They occur in combination, and the combination of symptoms varies from person to person and within circumstances.

The following are some signs that, in combination, indicate depression in children and teens:

- Daily sadness, tears
- Expressions of hopelessness
- Decreased interest in life and decreased enjoyment of activities previously considered fun
- Decreased energy, sometimes accompanied by bursts of activity
- Isolation
- Appearing to shut down emotions completely
- Decreased self-esteem
- Increased feelings of guilt
- Sensitivity that becomes extreme and can result in hostility
- Complaints of innocuous ailments leading to increased school absences
- Sleep changes—sleeplessness or inability to get up in the morning

When you recognize a combination of these changes in your teen, you will get a sick feeling in your belly. Trust yourself when you think that something is very wrong. Then, do something about it. Seek the help of professionals.

Chapter 16

Keeping an Eye Out for the Glitter

What other job requires this kind of vigilance? Twenty-four hours a day, for as long as parents have been raising their children, they have been plagued by questions about their fitness for the job. Thanks to the plethora of parenting advice (yes, the irony) out there, parents can be led to question every small decision they make. Do I ignore this behavior? Do I hire a tutor or a nanny or a special coach or a parenting expert? Does he need medication or more time outside? Am I missing something? Is she keeping secrets? What am I seeing? What am I doing?

You *can* learn to trust yourself through the process, understanding that moments of doubt and fear are part of the deal. The doubts can't be allowed to drive your decisions, though. Nor can they be allowed to freeze you in your tracks. You *can* make reasoned choices and decisions based on your own values and a desire to raise your young to be people of character, kindness, and contribution. If you are willing to rely on your good instincts and listen to advice from trusted people who care about you and your children, you and yours will be fine. Knowing that you will make plenty of mistakes and that no mistake is the whole story, you can continue to work at being the best parent you can be.

The truth is your children will always need you to be their parent. These kids of yours, even when they are grown and have children of their own, will need you. When you signed on, you signed on for your lifetime. So decide to fight for what is right and fair, and your children will learn to do the same. Challenge the culture of victimhood, and emphasize the truth of freedom and choice given to each of us, and your children will learn to be accountable. Acknowledge that all the small things you choose to do each day and all those things you choose to ignore come together to form character, and your children will learn the importance of choosing.

As you work on becoming a better parent, you become a better person right in front of your children. They will see that a poor choice can be balanced out by a brave one and that you are in charge of how you fix your mistakes. They will see that you choose to see life optimistically and that you are grateful for the life you have. They will see how you treat others and how you react to the way others treat you.

Acknowledge that all people, even you, have bad moments, but emphasize that they are only moments. Those five bad minutes in the morning must not be overestimated. They can't be allowed to dictate the whole day. They can be put into perspective, and your child can still have a great, productive day. Poor choices and bad moments are only a part of the story, and they only become the story if they are not addressed and then left behind. Your child can learn from every single poor choice. He can combine the excellent things he does and the strong moves he makes to write his growing story.

Sometimes *no* is the right word to say to a child. Sometimes explanation is unnecessary. This may not be well received in the moment, but that doesn't mean it's not right for the moment. Madeline Levine said, "If you can't stand to see your child unhappy, you are in the wrong business."[1] Your kids aren't supposed to love everything you do. They develop their strong spirits and their own values by pushing up against your rules, and they are reassured in their quest for character by the fact that you don't crumble at every slammed door and stomped foot.

If you are frustrated with unrelenting demands from your children, if it seems they are constantly asking for one more thing, one more outing, one more bend to the rules, one more friend over, one more dessert, one more video game, then you need to know your children want you. They want your time and your attention. They want to know you see them where they are. They need to feel connected to you, and they need to know they are understood and loved unconditionally by you, in this moment and over the long haul. They need to feel safe—physically and psychologically. They need you. So skip the exotic trips, the expensive toys, the privileges and indulgences. Take time to talk and listen, to sing and dig in the dirt, to read a book together. That's what they want. It's not too much. You signed up for this.

From a very young age, children search for the meaning behind things. As they grow up, they seek meaning in their very lives. They instinctively know that there is more to this than getting good grades, going to a good college, partying, and getting a high-paying job. They are desperate to find the higher purpose. They know that love for neighbor and service to neighbor are always connected. It's your job to reinforce what they already know.

Your family is the first line of defense against a culture that diminishes life at every turn. You are fighting for the souls of the children you love in a hostile world. As you undertake this awesome responsibility, you may not always feel so great about the work. You may fail publicly, horrendously, hugely, but you can and must come back up off your knees and take the next step. You have to keep going, even if you're stumbling along, because the children need you. Trust yourself; trust the timing of your life; and, as a wise old woman would say, "You'll be fine."

What a choice you have made! When you decided to become a parent, you decided to hand your time, your best skills, your most brilliant ideas, your heart, and your soul over to the business of raising a child you could not possibly love more. You didn't realize, did you? And that child is incredible. She has imaginary friends who keep her company when she's lonely. She laughs as many as three hundred times a day. When she feels like crying out loud or giving a good scream, she does it. She is bright and beautiful, and her eyes can see right into your soul.

He wants violin lessons today and drum lessons tomorrow. He loves the chess club and climbs trees like a monkey. He asks for hugs when he's sad, and he gives them when he's glad. He swings higher and higher, and he slides faster and faster, unafraid to fall on his backside at the bottom. He can leave the remains of a chocolate ice cream cone on his face for an entire day and not be bothered by it at all. When he gives you a big smooch, your faces stick together for just a second, and you both laugh.

Children are recurring miracles, each and every one of them. How lucky you are to have the chance to be with yours, to guide, to struggle with, and to read to as he travels the road that is growing up! Your children decorate your life. He writes beautiful poems. She draws stunning pictures that you stick all over the refrigerator. He makes handprint plates, and she decorates valentines that say "I love yuo." They scatter glitter everywhere to remind you to look, to remember, to appreciate, and to smile.

Dear Parent,

Never forget that the glitter is out there and why it's there. Let it peek at you from your shirt sleeve or your cheek. Let it remind you to notice all the little things that make up this great life of yours.

The Lists

In a nutshell, these are some of the things you want your children to know how to do before they are adults, some important truths you want them to consider, and some advice to share with them.

Your child should know how to do these things before he is grown. He will not learn them without a teacher. If you don't know how to teach these skills, then find someone who can help you and join in on the lesson yourself:

- How to make hospital corners when making the bed
- How to set their own alarm
- How to mow the lawn
- How to add and subtract in her head
- How to act at a funeral and a wake
- How to introduce himself and how to introduce his friends to adults
- How to set a table for both casual dinner and formal dinner and which fork to use for what
- How to ride a bike and change a bike tire
- How to measure tire pressure, put air in a low tire, and change a tire on the car
- How to read a map
- How to play cards and board games
- How to memorize and recite a poem
- How to tie shoelaces in a double knot and get it out
- How to find her own street on a map
- How to calculate time and mileage for a trip
- How to determine tip amounts
- How to write a personal letter, business letter, and thank-you note
- How to make a budget
- How to open a bank account
- How to get a library card and use it to borrow books

These are fifteen life lessons you will want to make sure your children have learned:

- There is a road for each of us to follow. No two people's journeys are quite the same.
- The body you've been given, whether you like it or not, is the only one you get, so take care of it.
- Excellence is a way of living.
- You can be a good person and still make a poor choice.
- If you want a kitten, start out by asking for a horse.
- It matters what you do.
- It matters how you think of yourself.
- There are people you know and people you will meet who struggle against incredible odds and continue to show up and try again and again. You can learn a lot from them.
- Everyone matters, and no one matters more than anyone else.
- There is great dignity in hard work—any kind of hard work.
- You are never too old to kiss your mom or hug your dad.
- The possibilities are endless. Do something that scares you.
- If a friend offers you dope or a joint, then he is not your friend.
- It's hard to recover from a lie.
- When things get really hard and you feel like giving up, someone will reach out a hand. Someone will hold hope for you, so stay in the game.

Everyone knows that unsolicited advice is generally ignored. As parents, though, you have an advantage. Advice giving is your business. You can sneak your advice in between stories and fun and meals and walks on the beach. Over the years, you'll be able to share some pretty important advice with your children. If they don't seem to hear it today, then one day they will need it, and it will come back to them. Here are some examples:

- Do today well. Tomorrow will take care of itself.
- Read the directions, and then decide whether to follow them.
- Smile at strangers, and say hello to people.
- Not everything is a big deal, but some things are. Learn the difference.
- When someone criticizes you, listen to what they say, decide if there is truth in what they say, and act on it if there is.
- Always, always, always expect to be treated respectfully by boyfriends and girlfriends.
- Keep your promises.
- Keep an open mind and listen to people with whom you disagree.
- Stand up for what you believe in, and stand up for the little guy.

- Stand beside the person who has no one.
- Stand up straight and take your hands out of your pockets.
- If you don't understand the word, look it up.
- Don't quit. Be tenacious.
- If you see something wrong, then do something about it.
- Know the difference between needing something and wanting something.
- Find something worth fighting for, and fight to the end.
- Don't call names, and always fight fair, no matter what the politicians do.
- Hold the door. You're not in that big of a hurry.
- Give up your seat. You're young and healthy.

Notes

CHAPTER 1

1. Quoted in Mike Penner, "99 Things about John Wooden," *Los Angeles Times*, November 30, 2009, https://www.latimes.com/archives/la-xpm-2009-nov-30-la-sp-mike-penner4-30-2009nov30-story.html.

CHAPTER 8

1. Michael Gurian, *The Wonder of Boys: What Parents, Mentors, and Educators Can Do to Shape Boys into Exceptional Men* (New York: Putnam, 1996).
2. Douglas MacArthur, *Duty, Honor, Country: Two Memorable Addresses* (New York: Rolton House, 1962).

CHAPTER 9

1. Douglas MacArthur, *Duty, Honor, Country: Two Memorable Addresses* (New York: Rolton House, 1962).
2. birguslatro, "The Last of the Monsters with Iron Teeth," Carcinisation, October 4, 2014, https://carcinisation.com/2014/10/04/the-last-of-the-monsters-with-iron-teeth/.
3. Michael Gurian, *The Wonder of Boys: What Parents, Mentors, and Educators Can Do to Shape Boys into Exceptional Men* (New York: Putnam, 1996).

CHAPTER 11

1. Office of the Surgeon General, *Protecting Youth Mental Health: The U.S. Surgeon General's Advisory* (Washington, DC: U.S. Department of Health and Human

Services, 2021), https://hhs.gov/sites/default/files/surgeon-general-youth-mental
-health-advisory.pdf.

CHAPTER 14

1. Meg Schneider and Joan Zuckerberg, *Difficult Questions Kids Ask—and Are
Afraid to Ask—about Divorce* (New York: Simon and Schuster, 1996).
2. Schneider and Zuckerberg, *Difficult Questions Kids Ask.*

CHAPTER 15

1. Amanda Crowder, Tracy Elsenraat, Robert Hull, and Lisa Weed Phifer, *CBT
Toolbox for Children and Adolescents: Worksheets and Exercises for Trauma, ADHD,
Autism, Depression, and Conduct* (Eau Claire, WI: PESI, 2017).
2. Peg Rosen, "ADHD and Anxiety," Understood, accessed June 2020, https://www
.understood.org/en/articles/adhd-and-anxiety-what-you-need-to-know.
3. Rachel L. Hutt, *Feeling Better: CBT Workbook for Teens: Essential Skills and
Activities to Help You Manage Moods, Boost Self-Esteem, and Conquer Anxiety*
(Emeryville, CA: Althea Press, 2019).
4. Hutt, *Feeling Better.*

CHAPTER 16

1. Madeline Levine, "Raising Successful Children," *New York Times*, August
4, 2012. https://www.nytimes.com/2012/08/05/opinion/sunday/raising-successful
-children.html.

Bibliography

Beasley, Brett. "The Lost Virtue." *Notre Dame Magazine* (Summer 2019). https://magazine.nd.edu/stories/the-lost-virtue/.

Bennett, William J., ed. *The Book of Virtues for Young People: A Treasury of Great Moral Stories*. New York: Simon and Schuster, 1997.

birguslatro. "Last of the Monsters with Iron Teeth." Carcinisation. October 4, 2014. https://carcinisation.com/2014/10/04/the-last-of-the-monsters-with-iron-teeth/.

Bishop, Penny A., and Lisa M. Harrison. *The Successful Middle School: This We Believe*. 5th ed. Columbus, OH: Association of Middle Level Education, 2020.

Christakis, Erika. *The Importance of Being Little: What Young Children Really Need from Grownups*. New York: Penguin Books, 2016.

Churchill, Winston. *The Gathering Storm*. Boston: Houghton Mifflin, 1948.

Coyle, Daniel. *The Talent Code: Greatness Isn't Born. It's Grown. Here's How*. New York: Bantam Books, 2009.

Crowder, Amanda, Tracy Elsenraat, Robert Hull, and Lisa Phifer. *CBT Toolbox for Children and Adolescents: Worksheets and Exercises for Trauma, ADHD, Autism, Depression, and Conduct*. Eau Claire, WI: PESI, 2017.

Frankel, Lois P. *Nice Girls Don't Speak Up or Stand Out: How to Make Your Voice Heard, Your Point Known, and Your Presence Felt*. New York: Grand Central Publishing, 2020.

Giannetti, Charlene C., and Margaret Sagarese. *The Roller-Coaster Years: Raising Your Child through the Maddening yet Magical Middle School Years*. New York: Broadway Books, 1997.

Gibson, Caitlin. "Why Aren't Teenagers Driving Anymore?" *Washington Post*, February 21, 2023.

Gilligan, Carol. *In a Different Voice: Psychological Theory and Women's Development*. Cambridge, MA: Harvard University Press, 2016.

Gurian, Michael. *The Wonder of Boys: What Parents, Mentors, and Educators Can Do to Shape Boys into Exceptional Men*. New York: Putnam, 1996.

———. *The Wonder of Girls: Understanding the Hidden Nature of Our Daughters*. New York: Pocket Books, 2002.

Gurian, Michael, Kathy Stevens, Patricia Henley, and Terry Trueman. *Boys and Girls Learn Differently! A Guide for Teachers and Parents.* San Francisco: Jossey-Bass, 2001.

Hansen, Sharon A. *Executive Functioning Workbook for Teens: Help for Unprepared, Late, and Scattered Teens.* Oakland, CA: Instant Help Books, 2013.

Hicks, Marybeth. *Bringing Up Geeks: How to Protect Your Kid's Childhood in a Grow-Up-Too-Fast World.* New York: Berkley Books, 2008.

Holmes, Kelly. "Lists of Things to Say to Kids." Happy You, Happy Family. 2016. www.happyyouhappyfamily.com.

Hutt, Rachel L. *Feeling Better: CBT Workbook for Teens: Essential Skills and Activities to Help You Manage Moods, Boost Self-Esteem, and Conquer Anxiety.* Emeryville, CA: Althea Press, 2019.

Levine, Madeline. "Raising Successful Children." *New York Times*, August 4, 2012. https://www.nytimes.com/2012/08/05/opinion/sunday/raising-successful-children.html.

MacArthur, Douglas. *Duty, Honor, Country: Two Memorable Addresses.* New York: Rolton House, 1962.

Mader, Jackie. "The Complex World of Pre-K Play." Hechinger Report. November 15, 2022. https://www.hechingerreport.org/the-complex-world-of-pre-k-play/.

Newberger, Eli H. *The Men They Will Become: The Nature and Nurture of Male Character.* Reading, MA: Perseus Books, 1999.

Office of the Surgeon General. *Protecting Youth Mental Health: The U.S. Surgeon General's Advisory.* Washington, DC: U.S. Department of Health and Human Services, 2021. https://hhs.gov/sites/default/files/surgeon-general-youth-mental-health-advisory.pdf.

———. *Social Media and Youth Mental Health: The U.S. Surgeon General's Advisory.* Washington, DC: U.S. Department of Health and Human Services, 2023. https://hhs.gov/sites/default/files/sg-youth-mental-health-social-media-advisory.pdf.

Penner, Mike. "99 Things about John Wooden." *Los Angeles Times*, November 30, 2009. https://www.latimes.com/archives/la-xpm-2009-nov-30-la-sp-mike-penner4-30-2009nov30-story.html.

Reichert, Michael, and Richard Hawley. *Reaching Boys, Teaching Boys: Strategies That Work and Why.* San Francisco: Jossey-Bass, 2016.

Rideout, Victoria, Alanna Peebles, Supreet Mann, and Michael B. Robb. *The Common Sense Census: Media Use by Tweens and Teens.* San Francisco: Common Sense Media, 2022. https://commonsensemedia.org/sites/default/files/research/report/8-18-census-integrated-report-final-web_0.pdf.

Ripley, Amanda. *The Smartest Kids in the World: And How They Got That Way.* New York: Simon and Schuster, 2013.

Roberts, Walter B., Jr. *Working with Parents of Bullies and Victims.* Thousand Oaks, CA: Corwin Press, 2008.

Rosen, Peg. "ADHD and Anxiety." Understood. Accessed June 2020. https://www.understood.org/en/articles/adhd-and-anxiety-what-you-need-to-know.

Rotter, Julian B., June E. Chance, and E. Jerry Phares. *Applications of a Social Learning Theory of Personality.* New York: Holt, Rinehart and Winston, 1972.

Sax, Leonard. *Girls on the Edge: Why So Many Girls Are Anxious, Wired, and Obsessed—and What Parents Can Do.* 2nd trade paperback ed. New York: Basic Books, 2020.

———. "Parenting in the Age of Awfulness." *Wall Street Journal*, December 17, 2015. https://www.wsj.com/articles/parenting-in-the-age-of-awfulness -1450397051.

Schneider, Meg, and Joan Zuckerberg. *Difficult Questions Kids Ask—and Are Afraid to Ask—about Divorce.* New York: Simon and Schuster, 1996.

Shepard, Lorrie A., and Mary Lee Smith. "Escalating Academic Demand in Kindergarten: Counterproductive Policies." *Elementary School Journal* 89, no. 2 (November 1998): 135–45. https://www.journals.uchicago.edu/toc/esj/1988/89/2.

Simmons, Rachel. *Odd Girl Out: The Hidden Culture of Aggression in Girls.* Rev. and updated ed. New York: Mariner Books, 2011.

Sockolov, Matthew. *Practicing Mindfulness: 75 Essential Meditations to Reduce Stress, Improve Mental Health, and Find Peace in the Everyday.* Emeryville, CA: Althea Press, 2018.

Vance, Erik. "The Secret to Raising a Resilient Kid." *New York Times*, September 1, 2021. https://www.nytimes.com/2021/09/01/parenting/raising-resilient -kids.html#:~:text=Build%20a%20stable%2C%20safe%20foundation.&text =Children%20need%20to%20feel%20they,she's%20loved%20no%20matter%20what.

Vogt, Susan. *Raising Kids Who Will Make a Difference: Helping Your Family Live with Integrity, Value, Simplicity, and Care for Others.* Chicago: Loyola Press, 2002.

We Are Teachers Staff. "Lawnmower Parents Are the New Helicopter Parents and We Are Not Here for It." We Are Teachers. August 30, 2018. https://www .weareteachers.com/lawnmower-parents/.

Willingham, Daniel T. *Why Don't Students Like School? A Cognitive Scientist Answers Questions about How the Mind Works and What It Means for the Classroom.* San Francisco: Jossey-Bass, 2009.

Index

About the Author

Patricia McGann, an educator of more than thirty years, has degrees in nursing, counseling, and school administration. Her careers in psychiatric nursing; community counseling; teaching at the graduate, high school, and elementary school levels; school administration; and educational consulting provide the foundation for her unique perspective on raising children. Mrs. McGann has been married to Terrence for fifty-two years, and she has five adult children and fourteen grandchildren.